KICK THE
BALLS

KICK THE BALLS

An Offensive Suburban Odyssey

ALAN BLACK

HUDSON
STREET
PRESS

HUDSON STREET PRESS
Published by Penguin Group
Penguin Group (USA) Inc., 375 Hudson Street, New York, New York 10014,
U.S.A. • Penguin Group (Canada), 90 Eglinton Avenue East, Suite 700,
Toronto, Ontario, Canada M4P 2Y3 (a division of Pearson Penguin Canada
Inc.) • Penguin Books Ltd., 80 Strand, London WC2R 0RL, England • Penguin
Ireland, 25 St. Stephen's Green, Dublin 2, Ireland (a division of Penguin
Books Ltd.) • Penguin Group (Australia), 250 Camberwell Road, Camberwell,
Victoria 3124, Australia (a division of Pearson Australia Group Pty. Ltd.) •
Penguin Books India Pvt. Ltd., 11 Community Centre, Panchsheel Park, New
Delhi – 110 017, India • Penguin Group (NZ), 67 Apollo Drive, Rosedale, North
Shore 0632, New Zealand (a division of Pearson New Zealand Ltd.) • Penguin
Books (South Africa) (Pty.) Ltd., 24 Sturdee Avenue, Rosebank, Johannesburg
2196, South Africa

Penguin Books Ltd., Registered Offices: 80 Strand, London WC2R 0RL, England

First published by Hudson Street Press, a member of Penguin Group (USA) Inc.

First Printing, June 2008
10 9 8 7 6 5 4 3 2 1

REGISTERED TRADEMARK—MARCA REGISTRADA

HUDSON
STREET
PRESS

LIBRARY OF CONGRESS CATALOGING-IN-PUBLICATION DATA

Black, Alan.
  Kick the balls : an offensive suburban odyssey / Alan Black.
    p. cm.
  ISBN 978-1-59463-047-7 (alk. paper)
  1. Soccer—Humor. 2. Black, Alan. 3. Soccer for children—Coaching.
4. Suburbanites—United States. I. Title.
  GV943.2.B53 2008
  796.334—dc22   2008014301

Printed in the United States of America
Set in Palatino and Colossalis

This book is dedicated to the best trio in the world—
Ana, my wife, and Angela and Grant, my kids.

Contents

Preface   ix

A Note to the Reader   xiii

THE FIRST HALF

Chapter 1. Mac Allah   3

Chapter 2. The Kickoff   11

Chapter 3. Faith   20

Chapter 4. Defense   23

Chapter 5. Strictly Speaking   43

Chapter 6. Multicultural Nuts   49

Chapter 7. On the Offensive with the Tribe   56

Chapter 8. Who Are You?   68

Chapter 9. Joining the Suburbanites   78

Chapter 10. Body Parts   89

Chapter 11. New Seeds   94

Chapter 12. Good Coach   103

HALFTIME

Chapter 13.   Going South   111

THE SECOND HALF

Chapter 14.   Back to the Front   127

Chapter 15.   Cursed   131

Chapter 16.   Hooligans   142

Chapter 17.   Moms   148

Chapter 18.   Atmosphere   155

Chapter 19.   Injuries   164

Chapter 20.   Help   172

Chapter 21.   Fair and Balanced   182

Chapter 22.   All Change   191

Chapter 23.   No Substitute   200

Chapter 24.   Green   205

Chapter 25.   Make Believe   209

Chapter 26.   Saturday   215

Chapter 27.   The Chosen Few   224

Chapter 28.   The Emptiness   229

Chapter 29.   The Pizza Party   243

EXTRA TIME

Born Again on the Fourth of July   251

Acknowledgments   255

About the Author   257

Preface

As a boy, I knew a man called Mr. Roberts. He was a bastard. Also, his house blew up, and I was happy about it. It made the national news. GAS EXPLOSION DESTROYS HOUSE IN GLASGOW, SCOTLAND. Karma: Mr. Roberts had paid the price for his biased refereeing.

My team of ten-year-olds was playing against his son's team. I was team coach, team captain, and loudmouth. We were born from the takings at numerous garage sales. We had trawled the neighborhood asking grannies and mums to donate any old junk to the cause of building our neighborhood team. Finally, we'd raised enough money to buy soccer uniforms with a Glasgow crest weaved into the chest. The city's bizarre emblem of the bird that never flew, the tree that never grew, the bell that never rang, and the fish that never swam was stitched proudly above our hearts. Before each game we would hold our uniforms to our mouths and kiss them passionately.

"We'll die for this," I yelled, and the team unanimously agreed.

This was the way we played our soccer. It was more important than life or death.

The game against Roberts's squad began with travesty and ended worse. Mr. Roberts himself had decided to referee the game when the neutral selection had failed to show. From the kickoff, it was obvious he was favoring his son's team. My cursing and swearing were well known but on this fateful night they reached new heavens. With fifteen minutes left in the game, and the score tied at zero–zero, I made a brilliant sliding tackle to deny his team a goal-scoring opportunity. Roberts blew his whistle shrilly and reached for his red card.

"*Off!*" he bawled into my face, his spittle forming at the mouth like on a rabid dog.

"Fuck off," I screamed.

But he was a foot taller, an adult, and had me by the scruff of the neck. I struggled free, pulled off my uniform, and threw it in his face, whereupon he stamped it into the mud; the bird that never sang was obliterated by muck. I picked it up, kissed the badge, and walked off. My team was burning with fury. Minutes later, we scored the greatest goal never seen by most of mankind.

Mr. Roberts wasn't done, and somehow awarded his son's team an undeserved penalty kick in the last minute of the game. Despite a valiant attempt by our goalkeeper, the enemy scored to tie. As we left the field, heading back to our neighborhood, I turned and yelled at Mr. Roberts, "One day you'll fucking pay for this!"

Three years later, he returned home from work and found

his house scattered across the street. The curse had worked, even though the bastard hadn't been home when the explosion happened. I vowed then to take the magical elixir of curses into my armory for the future.

I knew I would need them.

•   •   •   •

Three decades later, thousands of miles from the cold fields of Glasgow, a strong sun whipped the back of a Saturday morning in a suburb near San Francisco. Here I was, the new assistant coach to the Dragons, a team of under-nine suburban kids setting out for the first time on the field of dreams. The head coach was a guy called Mahmoud, an Iranian who had escaped the rotten mullahs of Eye-Ran. Both our sons were on the team. The winds of history had plopped an Iranian and a Scot in the golden California suburbs, our paths crossed at the junction of the soccer field.

And now on that very field I was listening to a soccer referee issue a warning. He was dressed in coward's yellow. "Last year a fistfight broke out between parents and coaches. The police were called and arrests were made. You must remain in control. Safety and order are the top priorities for the league. You will be banned from coaching if there is any trouble."

I looked at the car park and wondered which car was his. Must be the Volvo, I thought. Safety first.

"No fatwas against the referee," I said to Mahmoud. We came from nations with long traditions of kicking balls until it hurt.

A Note to the Reader

Some names and identities have been changed to protect the guilty. A little timing manipulation helped the flow of the story, and some conversations were sharpened. That said, it's time for kickoff.

THE FIRST
HALF

CHAPTER 1

Mac Allah

San Francisco apartments had been home for a decade but now my urban living was over. No more listening to the neighbor chop a line of cocaine on her coffee table in the apartment above. No more enduring the freak vacuuming below me at three a.m. No more suffering the exercising lump of blubber next door shaking my bed at six a.m. as she sweated to Richard Simmons tapes.

I was past it. I was ready to be suburban.

My job was still in the city, though. Five days a week, I earned my crust pouring drinks in a bar in a badass neighborhood where the homeless camped, the abusers fiddled, the destitute wandered, and the glamorous street prostitutes in their tight-fitting dresses did their best to hide their Adam's apples and bollocks. Moving to the suburbs was my escape from this American horror show. My family had space, a mortgage, a healthy lawn, a view of the hills, and a lavatory that did not share smells with a neighbor across the air shaft. Garage sales happened, and gardeners clipped bushes. There were block parties. The local police handed out trading cards of themselves in their uniforms. The fire station had an annual pancake breakfast for the kids. There was a smile in the street, and when people said hello to you, they were not asking for a quarter.

My realtor had said, "Now you're living in the suburbs, what are you going to do to contribute to your suburban community?"

"I'm going to run for mayor and I am going to win," I replied.

"Maybe you should try something else first," she said. "Get to know people, see how they live out here, what they like, what's important to them. Maybe you should coach little league or something. That's a good place to start."

"That's a good idea. Little league," I said, sensing that it was perhaps the perfect opportunity for me to find my peace in the multicultural suburban jigsaw.

Little league coaching got you a medal for volunteering in suburban America. Americans valued the coach like they valued massacring turkeys in November. There was Madden at Oakland, Paterno at Penn State, Torre at the Yankees, Jackson at the Bulls: legends all. They made men of boys. When they walked down Main Street, people simply referred to them as Coach.

Now it was my turn: I was going to help fashion the Dragons into a winning team. I was going to instill in them the virtues of victory. That was the American way. That was also my way. The parents would admire me and say, *He's got what it takes.* The social campaign would be off to a good start with a winning season and many handshakes. It would be a solid first step toward the mayor's office.

I looked to my past for inspiration, coaches I'd known as a kid in Scotland. A beast came to mind. Mr. Gibson ran his team like a guard taking care of prisoners at Abu Ghraib. He used a weapon of humiliation called the Crook. During a game, I'd be running full speed down the sideline chasing the ball. Without warning, my head would be mostly sheared off by Gibson's crook. I'd collapse on the sideline gasping for air. Gibson would give me a poke with his toe to check that I wasn't dead.

"You're finished today, son," he'd whisper in my ear, the good shepherd that he was.

In a nation of men with shriveled chests and puny shoulders, Gibson was the anomaly, the rank opposite. He was the Arnold Schwarzenegger of Scotland. He had steel sinews that caged his abdomen. A disciplined mustache sat on his lip, each hair iron rigid. He was fond of saying to kids,

"You're fucking shite."

The only loss Coach Gibson experienced was his stomach. Rumor had it that cancer gnawed it to the bone, ate his muscles like cereal, and put him in a box.

There was no funeral. He just disappeared.

●　●　●　●

A paperboy on a bicycle delivered the paper to my new home. I picked up my mail from my old-fashioned mailbox nailed to a post with a decorative bird on top that looked like a cuckoo. Offers from companies selling hardwood floors, house insurance, new windows, foundation strapping in the event of an earthquake, and gardening businesses that would keep the homestead spick-and-span. The sky was big; the sun bathed in its bath of blue. The sidewalks were clean, my lawn green. I breathed in the fresh air of the day. But the morning headlines spoiled my eggs Benedict—

REFEREE ATTACKED BY PARENT

DAD KILLS DAD AT KIDS' GAME

SOCCER MOM THROWS SOY LATTE IN COACH'S FACE

The day didn't get any better—just getting to the field for the first practice of the Dragons' season pushed my rage gauge to Saudi summer temperatures. Traffic had been a blocked coronary artery, making the cartilage in my knee ache from continually depressing the clutch and shifting gears. The citizenry sat in blocked lanes for hours after standing in line at the post office, supermarket, ATM, the vending machine. It was as if the late Soviet Union had willed its famous lines to American freedom. Waiting was for Communists! No wonder the nation was burning fury faster than a barrel of crude. And then we took our kids to little league.

When I finally arrived, my first order of business was to bond with Coach Mahmoud. We were each a leg in the coaching pants, and we were strangers. We spun balls on our feet trying to impress each other with our skills. I fired some shots at the goal. Mahmoud kept the ball in the air with his head, then dropped it to his feet and fired a cannonball shot high over the crossbar and into the street, where it smashed off what looked like a Lexus.

Eventually we stopped, and simply stood with our arms folded. A plane flew over. I watched its trail for a minute, transfixed. Finally, I spoke.

"Winning is everything," I said, "especially in America. This isn't the place to be a loser. What do you think, Mahmoud?"

"Yes," he replied.

Was he conversationalist of the year, or what? I managed to get out of him that he was a computer guy, tech heavy, educated, a man who understood day trading. His wardrobe shrieked JCPenney. And because he was bearded, Middle Eastern, dark-skinned, and dressed in the camouflage of Dockers, the sentinels of the war on terror inevitably selected him from the line at airport security.

"They pick me out," he said.

"It's the pants," I said. "Very suspect."

He didn't find that funny. The war on Dockers was lethal.

Obviously, slacks were not going to be the stitch that bonded us together. A shared historical sporting moment between our nations offered a better shot at getting off on the right track. Soccer in revolutionary Iran had suffered greatly under the ayatollahs. Besides hurting sales of Bic razors, the revolution scorned the spontaneous emotions that thrived in soccer stadiums. The singing of secular soccer chants at games in Iran was discouraged. New songs were invented:

Death to America! Death to Israel! Death to the Infidel! Death to Overuse of the Back Pass!

But before all this hatred, before the munch of cancer swallowed his peacock throne, the Shah's last stand at preserving the credibility of his corrupt regime had centered around the 1978 soccer World Cup Finals in Argentina. The Shah's generous and humble nature was best exemplified in the rumor that he was offering a brand-new Rolls-Royce to any player who scored a goal during the tournament. The team was to be given a large sum of money if they could win a match. If they miraculously won the World Cup, the Shah would arrange for heavenly intervention and sort them out with an eternal supply of virgins and many riches for their families.

Iran had never previously qualified for the World Cup Finals. In Las Vegas they were considered 1,000-to-1 outsiders to win the Cup. In the first round of the tournament, they were drawn against Scotland, a team composed of limited talent, alcoholics, and dental disasters.

The entire Scottish nation believed we would win the World Cup and be the greatest country in the world. My mum pulled down a dusty globe and pointed to this strange country called Iran. There it was, way down in the hot parts, near the camels that were printed on the Arabian Peninsula.

"Easy meat. We'll beat them," said the Scotland team coach, chewing on his bacon sandwich hours before the match. The media were confident that European civilization could crush any team from the sandpit. Only a few members of the press corps noticed the trash receptacles from the Scotland team's hotel bar overflowing with the drained empties of every liquor bottle that the hotel possessed.

On the day of the match, Ayatollah Khomeini was in exile in his Paris apartment plotting the end of shaving. My mum moved a mountain of laundry to her feet, and set up her ironing board altar in front of the TV. My brother and I drank soda filled with enough sugar to rot dentures. We jumped on the sofa, screaming, "Scotland! Scotland!" until burps laid us out.

The whole nation tuned in, as did much of the rest of the universe. It was the World Cup, after all, the greatest sporting spectacle on the planet. Meanwhile, in the dressing rooms of the stadium in Argentina, Scottish players rubbed their temples and swallowed extra-strength aspirin by the handful. This was it—the clash of civilizations. Iran versus Scotland; Farsi versus Farcical.

Scotland scored first. Or more accurately, Iran scored an own goal. We were grateful, as the Scotland team seemed to be incapable of standing up and threading two passes together. Several of the players looked as if they were still drunk from the night before, and those who seemed more alert had a hair-of-the-dog look about them. The game dragged on like a severe hangover. With the score at one–zero and the game clock ticking down, I prayed that the superior European inebriates would escape with a victory through the proverbial back door. Then, Iran's #10 gathered the ball, sped through the hangovers, waltzed through the wrecked Scottish defense, and struck the ball under the stumbling goalkeeper into the back of the net.

My mum burned a shirt from the shock. I could hear the engine start on a new Rolls-Royce. Virgins across Iran trembled. Back at the World Cup, with only seconds to go in the game, the Scottish people and the world witnessed the national team collapse into volleys of bitter recrimination. Players pointed and yelled at each other, *Fuck you,* and *Fuck off.* The Scottish team coach placed his head in his hands as the referee blew the final whistle. Cemented in the national consciousness was the spit and hatred that rained down on the team from the Scotland fans who had mortgaged their homes to take the bus to Argentina.

My brother and I were so filled with disgust that we immediately converted to Islam.

"A-llah! A-llah! A-llah!" we shouted in our Scottish brogues, the Ayatollah unaware in his fancy Paris apartment that the Islamic Revolution was breaking out in Bonnie Scotland. My mother quietly stopped ironing and slapped my sibling on the butt with a clog. Me she ignored.

The day after the match, when newspapers were calling for public execution of the Scotland team, we learned the Iranian #10's name: Daniafard. He'd become the first Iranian to score a goal for his country in the World Cup Finals.

"Do you remember Argentina 1978," I said to Mahmoud in the bonding moment, "and that player number ten . . . ?"

"Daniafard," he said, with a huge fucking grin. So we stood united by the name of an obscure Iranian soccer player who may or may not have made it out of Iran with his new Rolls-Royce.

CHAPTER : 2

The Kickoff

My son was now ready to embark on his soccer journey. Since he was a baby, I had showered him in the game. His pajamas were covered in soccer balls, he had sat with me and watched hours of it on television, he had learned to shout mindless invective at the screen, he had heard all my childhood anecdotes of soccer adventure, and he could sport a Scottish accent when it came to cheering for Scotland. Best of all, he didn't like England.

Every dad dreamed of the glory of the son. I had high hopes for mine. One day he would lift the World Cup for the United States. It would be the proudest day of my life, sitting in the best box seats at the stadium for the World Cup Final, surrounded by the retired legends of the game. Pelé would shake my hand; Maradona would offer me a line of powder; Cruyff would do his turn for me; Éric Cantona would headbutt me, but lovingly. The television would air a soft-focus feature on me as the reason for my boy's greatness. Jim Nantz would be wet-eyed during the halftime break.

But for now, it was a wet Sunday afternoon. I was standing outside the local school auditorium in a long line of suburban parents keen to get Junior started in little league soccer, it being the healthy alternative to Harry Potter addiction and/or drug abuse. The line was moving like a slug stuck in a sea of salt. The registrars required triplicate copies of birth certificates, health insurance cards, inoculations, and evidence of shin guard ownership. Oh, and parental details.

"This is worse than the post office," I said to the man behind me.

"Worse than waiting at immigration," he replied.

"Now, that is bad," I said. "I waited in the wrong line for four hours to get an appointment for a citizenship test, and then I had to come back the next day and wait another four hours in the correct line."

"Did you pass the test?" he asked.

"Nearly. I got all the questions about America right. The hard stuff, like what is the capital and who the fuck was George Washington? All that rubbish. But when it came to the last question, I failed."

"What was it?"

"Have you ever been arrested for a crime?"

"And?"

He squinted his eyes and looked at me closely. Children were running around.

"I told them the truth. I got done for selling alcohol to a minor."

Here, the guy took a small step backward. I ignored this and continued.

"Now I want to coach little league. I figured I could bring my soccer background from Scotland and help steer a team to victory. And it will help me bond with my son. I want him to grow up and be a professional soccer player."

The man was still squinting at me, and I was afraid I'd said something wrong. So I said, "What about you?"

"I work for the league," he whispered, and walked away.

Okeydokey.

My one incident of youth corruption happened during the soccer World Cup Finals in 1998. Blinded by TV coverage of a game that brought back memories of my childhood—a game in which the imperialist United States was beaten two–one by the now-even-more-rabid Iran—I heard a voice in the crowd shout out a fateful word: "Budweiser!" Without looking, I snapped the cap, handed over the bottle, and then watched as three police officers marched behind the bar, pulled out their badges, and said, "You are under arrest for selling alcohol to a minor." Standing on the other side of the bar was the plant, an Asian kid wearing a wire, who looked to be at least twenty-one. He had the bottle of Budweiser in his hand; he was smiling. Photographing, fingerprinting, processing me on the spot, the cops slapped down the court date and my boss showed me the red card and sent me home.

At the trial, the cops produced the wire, and the photograph of the corrupted youth. The judge asked, "How old is this young man?"

"Eighteen," said a cop.

"Eight-een?" repeated the judge, slowly, staring down at me with black-hatted contempt.

I hung my head in shame.

The bar got a $10,000 fine, and was closed for a month. I handed the State of California $800, reduced from $1,500, after I thanked the arresting police officer for pointing out to me the importance of keeping Budweiser out of the hands of America's youth. (He was right—for a start, it tastes like piss.)

When I finally became the head of the snake at the sign-up, I saw the league guy floating around among the volunteers behind the tables. I tried to smile at him but it came off as a weird sneer. I would not have been surprised if he'd rooted out my application and ended my coaching career before it started, disqualified for being a convicted corrupter of American youth.

No such luck. They handed me my registration. The die was cast.

The next step was to purchase the team uniform, the shorts, the socks, the shin guards, and the cleats. I was an Adidas man all the way; I had to have the three stripes. The choice of cleats, especially, was an important moment in any sporting life. Pulling on your cleats for a match was a precious moment, one that laced itself in the memory. Tying up the tongue, checking the studs, listening to the clatter of boots on the changing room floor. The stomach would flutter. The game beckoned. These were your magic boots that delivered speed. They were the leather that whacked winning shots at goal. And they were guards that protected you from the hack of another. I still had mine, worn through and battle scarred, from childhood. I would be buried with them.

My son was staring at the choices.

"Go for the Adidas," I said.

"No. I want the Puma."

"The Puma? Wrong choice."

"I don't care. I want the Puma."

He got the Adidas.

* * * *

Eventually, the day of the first game arrived. I got up early and had my prematch breakfast. I told my son he needed to eat a lot of protein and iron before playing, so we downed yogurt, juice, eggs, and a pint of Guinness. The gear was gathered and we headed off.

I drove to the field in my rotted '94 Mazda, unsafe at any speed. My son was crimson with embarrassment at the state of my car, especially when he saw his teammates arrive in the unmistakable rumble of the apocalypse—an army of new Suburbans and Explorers. All the little Dragons emerged looking swell in their new team uniforms: bright yellow tops with sky blue shorts, together giving the impression of a fantastic sunshine vacation; and if you squinted hard enough, they all turned green. Fancy, expensive kangaroo-leather cleats protected small toes, the bulging shin guards looked like casts. Gallons of Evian water were unloaded; organic oranges were cut open.

I said to a parent standing next to me, "You know that fancy French water? It comes from a toilet in Paris. They pretend it's from the Alps. Have you ever used a French toilet in a railway station? It's a hole in the ground. I got my foot stuck in one once and I had to get rescued. I didn't know the word for 'help.' Took ages to get me free. And they didn't have a toilet roll—thought I was in a third-world bog, to be honest."

"Can I help you?" he said.

"Er . . . I'm the team coach, the assistant." I stuck out my hand.

"Nice to meet you," he said, shaking my hand then wiping his on his jacket.

I looked up and the parents had gathered, ready to rah-rah-rah! This was the start of their children's participation in sports, a mandatory chapter in any parenting book of good standing. It was healthy, a building block for their children's social development. And I was partly responsible for nurturing it.

The first whistle of the season approached.

Mahmoud and I gathered our warriors.

Listen up!

We went over the game plan—play wide, cut inside, and mark up. As Mahmoud laid out the tactics, his words sunk like a body in quicksand. The players were not listening. Where were the Q-tips?

"I'm bringing wax remover to the next game," I told Mahmoud. "If that doesn't work, we'll drill holes."

He ignored me.

We went into the huddle and I gave the chant.

"One, two, three, four! Let them hear the Dragons roar! Who are ya?"

"The Dragons!"

"We're flying beasts!" I shouted. "Let's burn them alive, lads!"

Scorching human flesh may have been inappropriate as a motivational image for kids but soccer was serious business. It was a ruthless game. Toughness was vital.

I called up Tarzan. I beat my chest.

"Ah-a-ah—A-ahh—aha."

"What was that?" said Manny, one of our defenders.

"Tarzan," I said, "Don't you get Tarzan over here in America?"

"That doesn't sound like Tarzan," he replied, snuffling his snot. "That just sounds weird."

The boy had called me weird. I made an entry in my mental notebook. *Watch this cheeky wee bastard.*

And then, we were off and "running."

THE SPORTING GREEN

DRAGONS MAULED IN GAME 1

Opening day for the Dragons, and tomorrow can't come quick enough. This first performance was soccer psoriasis at its worst and that's only scratching the surface. Within ten minutes, the Dragons were losing by five goals. Their opponents swarmed them like locusts devouring Africa. Drake, the Dragons' goalie, would pick the ball out of the net twelve times by the end of the match.

The Dragons' defense vanished like light in a black hole. Jonathan, the left back, looked like a potted plant and played like one. Manny, the sweeper, persistently booted the ball toward his own goal in what seemed like a case of soccer suicide. His coaches yelled at him to stop; he answered with a blank stare. Sam, playing right defense, trundled with his arms stitched to his sides. Maybe his batteries needed changing. At the postgame press conference, Assistant Coach Black suggested that he have a lightning rod attached to his head in the hope that God would strike some electricity into him. The midfielders excelled in chewing gum and were absolutely rubbish. The Dragons' attackers were spectators. They never touched the ball.

As the goals piled up, the expression on the face of Drake, the Dragons' goalie, was that of a kid who had just discovered that Santa was a lie.

In the second half, the herding instinct came rushing to the surface as the Dragons attempted to hide behind each other. In their yellow tops they resembled a bunch of bruised bananas. The ball became a fearful object to be avoided. The Dragons' coaches could be seen aping up and down the line, flipping hands upward, turning away in horror, and finally hanging their heads.

As the *Sporting Green* is a family newspaper and words like "absolutely fucking diabolical" cannot be used to describe the Dragons, we are reduced to saying that the team was rather poor on its first outing.

Fortunately for the Dragons, the *Sporting Green* was circulated only inside my head. After the final whistle and the shame of conceding a dozen goals, I stood among the parents, who were clapping loudly and happily swarming around their little champions of defeat.

"Well done! You guys were great," they cheered.

The parents formed an archway of hands. The little losers ran through to whoops and yelps. A train of useless talent emerged from the dark tunnel into the bright sunny day.

"Is this what it's going to be like?" I said to Mahmoud.

"Pray," he said.

CHAPTER 3

Faith

Bartending was good for the tips and stressful for much else. Bartenders were more than the people who served the drinks. We were psychiatrists dispensing medication; confidants hearing the world's deceptions; shoulders to cry on; dispensers of judgment; and, ultimately, God (*You're cut off*).

While the suburbs slept, I was in the shower at 2:45 a.m. scraping the layers of beer, whiskey, and carbonated Coke splatters off my skin. After drying off, I got myself a tub of Ben & Jerry's ice cream, a large can of Dutch lager, and a big bag of insomnia, and settled down to watch my nightly episode of *The Shepherd's Chapel*, a satellite broadcast of hard-core, commercial-free Evangelical Christianity from darkest Arkansas. I watched it every night at three a.m. without fail. I avoided commercial secular television in the wee hours. All those insomnia drug ads kept me awake worrying about why I was. Awake, that is.

Fortunately, the religionists in Arkansas offered a mild

tranquilizer to the sleepless—they called it Bible study. The theme music to the show was droning bagpipes that sounded as if they were being played underwater. Being Scottish, I felt that they were calling me.

"You'll learn something watching this," I said to Ben and Jerry. "You'll learn what it means to be a real American."

The bright star of the show was the robust Reverend Arnold Murray, a man in possession of a good Scottish name. He sat in a simple room at a desk with nothing but the Holy Book in his hands and a terrific big bust of an eagle at his shoulder. On occasion, to make certain that the viewers understood the mystery of God, the audio and visual sync was off, making it appear that the reverend was speaking in tongues.

His oddball son, Reverend Dennis, a man with a dodgy mustache and skin that resembled the bottom of a Kentucky Fried Chicken bucket, ably supported Dad in his mission by filling in from time to time. Tonight, Dennis was in the chair leading the Bible study and answering mail from the faithful. His glasses steamed up as he strained to decipher the terrible handwriting. These letters, from places like Brainard, Nebraska, and Dibble, Oklahoma, were, for me, the highlight of the show. Sentences ran on like biblical floods flowing over the abandoned wreckage of bad grammar rot. I thought I heard a viewer ask if shaving existed in heaven, as he didn't like beards. I wanted to join this important exercise in theological discernment. I pulled out the quill and wrote my own letter to the Arkansas minister.

Dear Reverend Dennis Murray,

I have recently moved to the suburbs from the great Sodom of America called San Francisco. I have a nice garden. The roses are white and a white cross of Jesus stands tall on the hill. I have beautiful grass out front and it is green. My question, Reverend, is this—will God provide a lawn mower in heaven for my house or should I arrange for a John Deere to be buried alongside me? I have also started to coach a little league team in soccer and I know that soccer is a game that Americans don't know and is foreign but is it a sin to coach a game that is from parts of the world that hate America?

Thank you for your time in reading my letter and I hope you read it out on the air and mention my name and best wishes to your father, Arnold.

Yours faithfully,
Alan Black

The triumvirate of Bible, Dutch lager, and Ben & Jerry's was finally starting to kick in. The bagpipes sounded even farther away. I accidentally flicked the remote and landed on another Evangelical planet, Pat Robertson's *700 Club.* When the phone rang at his house, you knew who was calling. As sleep tumbled from its cave and dawn's witches began to creep over the horizon of the television set, I pictured Terry Meeuwsen, Pat's voluptuous and mature assistant and former Miss America, running toward me in nothing but her pantyhose. The land of Nod let her in.

CHAPTER 4

Defense

"I'm in flames. Let me out!"

My wife, Ana, swatted me across the belly.

"Calm down," she said, remembering she liked me and stroking my forehead. "You're having a nightmare. What happened?"

"I was back in Scotland."

"That'll do it."

"No. It was the memory of a high school soccer match I once played in."

"Do you want to tell me about it?"

Playing road games for my high school team gave me the travel bug. There were plenty of scary moments, when you played against teams in the lands that time forgot, small towns in the hills above Glasgow that would get cut off when the snow blocked the roads in winter, places populated with remote and perverted minds, and nervous livestock.

One frigid Saturday morning, when the iceman had cometh, we played against a team named after a Catholic saint. We arrived at the chilling school, the changing rooms dark, missing lightbulbs and running water. Next door, we could hear our opponents singing at the top of their lungs. They were banging the walls with their brute fists, chanting, *You're going home in a fucking ambulance*. We were silent as we changed into our soccer uniforms, though there was a faint squeaking as our butts squeezed shut like Tupperware lids.

This particular school had placed its soccer field at an immeasurable distance from the nearest civilization, miles from the actual building and surrounded by large and scary trees. Our screams would not be heard. (The state hospital for the criminally insane was just beyond the trees, too—those screams we *could* hear.) As for our opponents, well, they had a reputation for intimidation, for cruel and unusual tackling methods, and for being general carvers of flesh. They smoked cigarettes during the game. We'd also heard they sniffed glue for their halftime snack.

Kickoff approached. We watched as this gang of eleven cavemen took up positions on their half of the field. There was no ball. We had warmed up with one, practicing shooting, passing, and heading, but they were simply staring at the ground or kicking the goalposts, and sometimes each other, violently. Their arms seemed longer than was normal, and suspiciously, some of them sported full beards, even though they were supposed to be fourteen years old. The air felt thin.

Shortly after the whistle set the game in gear, my marker tried to set fire to my soccer top with his cigarette. I saw his hand down his red shorts as I looked down to see the burning frizzle on my shirt.

"Don't fucking think about getting by me today," he said, blowing smoke in my face, "or I'll burn your fucking leg off."

The referee was also their coach, so they said, and as his vile shade moved across the park, our players trembled at the chance of his intervention. He blew every foul in favor of his mob. He got in the way of the ball, bumped into us, and handed out whispered threats. I wondered if he really was their coach. How could a coach engage in such an offensive and dangerous example to youth and allow a squad of teenagers to puff like Joe Camel during a game? It was more likely that the real match referee had been given an offer he couldn't refuse before we arrived, something along the lines of *Leave or die*. This referee was clearly the big brother of one of the players.

Our coach, a mild man more familiar with teaching physics than coaching soccer, tried to get through to the referee that something was not working as perhaps it ideally should. The referee's denial was both blunt and profane—seemed our coach should leave and copulate with himself. God knew if we'd even make it to the second half.

The other team's central defender, and team captain, had a scar that ran like the Nile from his cheek to his chin. Other than that, his face was volcanic with a Dead Sea of blackheads. He was the hard man, the brick shithouse battering his way through the trials of growing up. He had no will to win, only to destroy. He spoke like a deranged psycho killer. "Fucking kill him!" he suggested, as one of his minions sped across the field and punched a hole in one of our players.

Besides being the victim of arson, my legs were scythed regularly, like wheat at the harvest. After one particularly gruesome tackle, I knew how it felt to be an astronaut, floating free from the earth. And as I got up and looked at the perpetrator—a buzzing villain in red shorts—I could not have known the danger I would face a few minutes later when I ran through on to the ball and found myself advancing alone toward their goalkeeper.

Going through my head were the words *Please miss*. I swept the ball in a side arc that sailed over the advancing goalie, and watched it trace a line in the sky. It made a nice parabola; something our physics teacher coach would no doubt have appreciated, had he not been rendered dumb with fear.

Oh, fuck no, I thought. *It's going in the net.*

Behind me, I heard the snorts of wildebeests, hammering across the field to trample me to death. Then from out of nowhere a strong gust of wind came out of the north and blew the ball in a zany zigzag; the ball boomeranged back over my head and flew like a magic orb back up the field. I turned and saw the butts of the herd dissolve, chasing the ball into the distance.

I looked at the dark and sketchy sky.

"Thank you, God, for stopping that going in," I said, to no one in particular.

But it wasn't long before we started racking up goals

against the glue-sniffers. I knew then that the game was going to end in a bad way. There could be deaths.

At the final whistle, we changed from the school soccer team to the cross-country team, as we ran for our gear in the changing rooms and then straight for the bus. Punches and kicks chased us, cigarette butts flew past our heads, *Fucking kill them* was chanted. Our coach fired the ignition on our bus and we sped out through the gates just before these barbarians managed to close them. I looked back and saw the pockmarked captain mangle a curse and genuflect, the signal clear: *Return and you shall die.* We had escaped from those demented lands.

In Scotland, we called these types of people *bampots*. My high school had its quotient, too. At the top of the bampot pile was Bobe, his nom de guerre. He led an elite team of deranged individuals, the highest quality. His disciples included the extremely violent, the only slightly touched, and a Down syndrome kid he brought in from the outside, a boy named Billy. He terrorized civilization with his aching wails. Together, they were the type of hooligan mob who would surround a hairless grandpa waiting at a bus stop and attack him with screams of *Baldy! Baldy!* Then, as the victim reached for his handkerchief to wipe away his tears, Bobe's gang would relieve him of his fare. Or when they saw the neighborhood's thalidomide victim, with his stunted arms, they would mock him with the penguin dance.

One day, when Bobe crossed my path, stupidly I agreed for my soccer team to play his squad of bampots. When we arrived, we were horrified to find that a pit had been dug at the side of the field. Abandoned shopping carts, upturned, lay among nearby bushes. With Bobe's team hindered by a lack of soccer skill and other human abilities, they quickly abandoned the match, rounded us up, and marched us off to the pit. Some of my players fled, but I was held tight by a beast named Corky, a large-limbed specimen who would have been more at home in a glass case in the Natural History Museum. Cast into the pit, we were prisoners.

We had no idea what was coming; and then, it didn't matter anymore. Shopping carts started to rain down on us. Soon we were trapped under a cage of Safeway property. I looked up and saw Bobe and the Down syndrome gaze of Billy leaning over us. Billy's wild face popped with malice as the white clouds in the sky raced past his purple head. He wailed as he dumped old paint cans, metal bolts, and soiled newspapers on top of us.

He shouted down: "Die!"

I panicked, shouting, "Billy's going to kill us. He'll set fire to the pit!"

Fortunately, those who had escaped raised the alarm and some adults came and set us free. As we got out, we saw Billy roaming around, pointing at heaven.

"Cunt," he yelled, with fiery breath, presumably at God.

* * * *

Though the Dragons' first game had been a disaster, I didn't feel the need to dig them a pit and hurl shopping carts down on them. Yet. Instead, defense was top of our postmatch conference agenda. At the training field, Mahmoud and I huddled up against a highly combustible eucalyptus tree and glanced, nervously in my case, over to where the parents and players were waiting for us to fire up the session.

"Something needs to be done, Mahmoud. The defense is like a sieve. A hole in the bucket. It drove me crazy that no one listened to a word I said."

"You take charge of the defense," he said. "I'll concentrate on planning the attacks."

That sounded a bit dodgy to me, but Mahmoud took off to the far end of the training ground with the attackers, and I rounded up the defenders with my Scottish verbal lasso.

"Now, children, Ah'm gonnay be coaching you in defense," I said.

"What?" said Drake, the goalkeeper.

"Defense."

"But I'm the goalkeeper," he said.

"That's part of the defense," I replied.

"I want to be the goalkeeper," said the potted plant, Jonathan.

"No, he's the goalkeeper."

"But he's not defense," said Manny.

"Yes, he is."

"But defense is linebackers."

"No, that's football."

"But I thought you called this football," said Manny.

I paused; the mental note popped up again—*cheeky wee bastard*.

"It is. You kick the ball with your feet."

I felt a seethe coming on. I saw those headlines over my eggs Benedict flash before my eyes.

"Now, listen. Let's try some drills on you."

It was wrong to think of the dental version.

I laid out the cones, retrieved the balls, crouched down to speak to their faces, and fought down the urge to clip them around the noggin for not listening to anything I was saying. They fidgeted, belched, and messed around. I could feel the radar of the parents on me, spying, examining the looks on their children's faces, making sure nothing horrible was happening on the soccer field with an abusive coach who might turn out to be the cause of wet sheets being changed in the middle of the night. I smiled at the team but my brown Scottish teeth did not match the sparkling solar radiance of their polished parents. I would have to work on my gleam. As the Dragons trained, I pulled out a notebook and recorded some observations, trying to look professional.

GOALKEEPER: Drake

Looks like he's suffering from any number of attention deficit disorders.

Good around swimming pools—diving in the wrong direction.

Drake's dad: Rastafarian haircut—may just be a do rather than a religious statement. Encourage Drake to see himself as a Burning Spear defending the sanctuary. Definitely a Wailer. Moans constantly. Use weed metaphors for encouragement? Have to ask, why is the Rasta lad a goalie when pot is all about scoring? Dreadlocks and dreadful, must be some connection there. Mention the goalie pope, John Paul II, played in Poland, as strong as a prophylactic, regularly stopped penetration of his end. Bales of ganja burning bright. Have to lie. Tell the dad that the boy has potential.

To summarize: Goalie strengths—absolutely none.

DEFENDER, Right Back: Sam

Should be right back in a stroller, by the sound of his whine.

Looks like he needs electric shock therapy to get him moving. The dolt in need of a volt. Uncoordinated, like a sack of old rags stitched together. No lightbulbs working inside his head. Suggest he stand in a thunderstorm and ask for a direct hit.

To summarize: Dolt's strengths—his forehead could be used as road.

DEFENDER, Left Back: Jonathan

Looks like he has been left back in Precambrian soil, zero motor skills, looks like a fern. Is a fern! Needs to be pruned, aphids massacring roses, a thorn in my ass. Parent: mum has a poisonous face, like oil of vitriol.

To summarize: Plant's strengths—would look good in a flowerpot.

DEFENDER, Sweeper: Manny (Cheeky Wee Bastard)

Big feet for a kid . . . looks like he's ready for the army.

Keeps kicking the ball toward own goal. Smirk merchant. Talkback smart-ass. Will have to rent John Wayne movies to find appropriate line of communication. One, two, three, four, I love the Marine Corps.

To summarize: Cheeky Wee Bastard's strengths—with correct training, could flatten opponents.

DEFENDER, Center Half: Ashley?

Kind of fat, runs with his nose in air, ate candy during practice, think he's called Ashley, didn't hear name first time round, could be something else, must find out. Will call him Ashley until he complains. No doubt in later years, he'll find himself standing in front of the refrigerator at four a.m., ice cream in one hand, cookies in the other, potato chips stuffed under the triple chin, string cheese in the pajamas pocket, a can of soda stuffed down his underpants, a salami rolled into the folds of fat that orbit him like Saturn's rings and when unwilling to walk back to the cathode-ray tube, he will climb into the refrigerator and cover his entire body in peanut butter before shooting up insulin.

To summarize: Porker's strengths—will attract birds with the peanut butter.

All the defenders were, as Coach Gibson would have said, "fucking shite."

I hid the notebook in my pocket. If it fell into the wrong hands there would be trouble with parents and the league, a disgrace, and a stain on my otherwise immaculate reputation.

"Get over here!" I snapped. "All of you, shut up and pay

attention. I don't like the fact that you don't listen to me. I'm the assistant coach."

"We don't understand what you're saying!" they shouted.

"Ah'm speakin' friggin' English. Why don't yeez open yer ears and listen!"

The tongue-lashing sparked the dolt in need of a volt to life for a brief second, but the prehistoric fern let a tear tumble from his moist leaf. It splashed on the grass like an asteroid hitting the planet.

I looked up and saw his mum flash a fierce glance in my direction. My blood ran cold. The fern ran to her side. I imagined her moving toward me with a burning poker dipped in sulfuric acid until close enough to insert it sideways into my lower orifice.

"You made him cry by yelling," said Manny.

"And swearing," said "Ashley."

• • • •

Just what was it with this whining, moaning generation of kids? Why did every moment have to be a fluffy laundered downy cushion of positive comfort? Everything from fabric softeners on their clothes to daily shampooing of their hair had turned young boys into relatives of the soft toys that littered their bedrooms. They cried when they got a tiny scratch on their finger, and were rushed to the emergency room when they fell on their head. The American nation was in danger of masculine meltdown. John Wayne had been dead too long. It was time to dig him up. Softness for American boys had become a national embarrassment. And whining the voice of a generation.

Where I grew up, whiners suffered.

We had two brothers, the McHoos, in our street gang who were doppelgängers for Frankenstein's monster. These frightful siblings lacked a lot of human characteristics, including eyelashes. Their heads were shaped like medieval battering rams, and they used them to terrifying effect. They were useless at the game, but we brought them along with us to other neighborhoods as mascots, and as security. They also carried the kit.

People trembled when they saw the McHoos coming. Maybe this was because they'd walk with their arms out straight. They also made a show of bringing four large metal bolts with them, which they shared and held up to their necks at the coin toss before the game. I always let them make the call with the other team captain. I don't remember them losing a coin toss.

All through my idyllic childhood we were engaged in a struggle for soccer supremacy with another mob in the neighborhood, and they had been whining about our unfair tactics when it came to playing. Hacking their players to pieces was displeasing to them, for some reason.

One day, the McHoos had spent the morning working on a broth, digging in the earth, looking for the finest flavors. By noon, they had mixed up a Worm Stew McHoo, a mix of mud, juicy maggots, and mashed slugs, in a delicate puddle sauce.

But what to do with it?

"I know," said the youngest McHoo.

So we kidnapped the other team's captain and subjected him to a meal, pouring it into his ears, much like gravy in a boat. A war crimes tribunal would probably have described our actions as torture, a violation of the Geneva Convention on prisoners' treatment, but we didn't care. All that mattered was that it shut the victim up in the future when it came to whining about rough tactics while playing soccer.

At our next game against the poor guy's team, they got their revenge. During the match, my brother started to bleed, horror-movie style. His leg had been ripped asunder by something, leaving a scar that would stay forever.

"Stick some grass on it," I told him. "Stick a leaf on the wound. You'll be fine."

The blood was pooling in his cleat. He struggled on, but the squishy splurge of blood was now turning his lower leg into a ghastly mess. He collapsed, and the team got underneath him and carried him home. Blood dropped down on our heads. He kissed the badge on our team uniform before a taxi took him to the hospital. The stitches were deep and many.

It was never proven how the broken bottles got inserted into the soccer field. But it was either an act of evil or an act of God. Either way, this current generation would have sued someone. We never gave it a second thought—if you poured worms down a guy's ear, you could expect to get glassed.

How to impart such nuggets of moral wisdom to this lot? I had to try.

I took Manny aside after practice. I imagined I could hone his cheeky wee bastard personality into a productive clip. It could come in useful if he could direct it against opponents. And if I could get him to like me, he would be less likely to start a fire of criticism that might spread through the team and on to the parents.

"Hey, Manny," I said, speaking slowly, trying to scuff the edge off the brogue. "Do you remember 'Chim chiminey, chim chiminey, chim chim cher-ee' in *Mary Poppins*?"

"What?"

"You know. *Mary Poppins*, the movie."

"No."

"You've never heard of it?"

"No. Why?"

"Well, it's got a song in it about a chimney sweep."

"What's that?"

"You know, when kids climbed into chimneys to clean them? In the old days, in England."

"Why did they do that?"

"To clean them."

"Why were they dirty?"

"Because you set a fire and it made smoke and made the chimneys black."

"Like a barbecue."

"Like a barbecue."

"I don't want to clean it," Manny said, obliquely.

"I know. Listen, you are the sweeper in our team."

"I don't want to be the sweeper."

"No, that's just the name of the position you're playing in the team. You're the sweeper."

"No. I don't want to be that, I don't like barbecues."

The Dickensian sooty chimney reference was not going to work out here in clean California, and I did not entirely entertain the notion of deriving satisfaction in stuffing Manny down one. That would be wrong. I would have to search for a better cultural reference, one a young American would grasp and appreciate. War.

"Manny, this is your position in the team. You are the most important defender we have. When you see the bad guy running toward you with the ball at his feet, run at him as if you are a tank and smash him out of the way. This is what the sweeper does. Think of him as a bad guy."

"Like the Indians."

"No, not like the Indians. They're not the bad guys."

"But they were against the cowboys."

"Look. Forget the good guys and the bad guys. Just try and get the ball off them."

"Off who?"

I gave up. The other central defender, who may or may not have been called Ashley, wandered close.

He was a kid who had a wimpy name, not to mention a preternatural ability to sniff out food at a hundred paces.

"Try and smell danger as it approaches you on the field. Think of it as a meal. Pretend that the attacker is someone to be eaten—and spat out," I added, in case he took my metaphor too seriously. He looked at me as if I were mad.

What could I do? Should I consider bringing two dozen Krispy Kreme donuts to the game and let Ashley eat them before the kickoff? It might get him interested, though we'd have to have a break before we played so he wouldn't puke them back up. Maybe I was on to something; maybe we shouldn't, after all, have a break—what attacker would want to visit our half of the field if it was liberally covered in vomit?

But no. I couldn't do that to a kid. The news had been filled in recent weeks with the story of a little league coach who wanted to get rid of a player from his squad, so he got one of his other players to clobber the victim with a metal baseball bat.

Why couldn't Ashley just play baseball?

If I'd had anything about me I would have confronted his parents. I could be sensitive. I ran the speech through my head:

"Mr. and Mrs. Whatever Your Names Are, here's the thing. Your son is fat—your fault—he's rubbish—his fault—and he has a stupid name—see point one. Don't bring him back."

But they had paid the fees to the league to have their boy coached, not abused.

That said, it troubled me greatly seeing fat kids huffing and puffing chasing a ball, not having any fun. It brought to mind a 1970s hula hoop that, when spun on the hips, let loose a peppermint aroma. Soccer ball manufacturers needed to think along those lines. We needed a ball that emitted food smells when kicked. The fast food–smelling ball could bring millions of fat people into the joy that is the game. Imagine it: the cross comes over, and as the player rises to head it into the net, a great whiff of Coca-Cola or a blast of chocolate ice cream or the burst of french fries would rocket up into the air, where it would lie like a happy miasma over the field. And soon, the food lover would be desperate to get near the ball, happily chasing it, losing the pounds.

With this in mind, I said to the kid who was maybe called Ashley, "What do you like to eat?"

"Ice cream," he said.

"Okay. When you see the ball, think of it as a big ball of mint chocolate chip rolling toward you, and you have to get to it first to put it back in the cone."

"It would be dirty."

"No. It's—erm—oh, shite, it doesn't matter. Just get the ball. Look, kid, you're a good player—"

"No, I'm not," he said.

I was about to give up for good when Mahmoud crept up.

"Mahmoud," I said, "do you like flying?"

"What?"

"Do you like to fly?"

He made a slight grimace. "I don't think about it. I just do it."

"Do you ever stop and stare at the trails of the planes disappearing into the blue?"

"No. How is the defense shaping up?" he asked.

"The defense? Like good geometry," I lied. "Organized,

straight, and sharp. Some of the boys have a hard time understanding my accent, though."

"Try an American accent."

This seemed a bit rich, coming from him.

"How is the offense looking, Mahmoud?"

"Good. On Saturday, we'll score."

I liked his confidence.

In the car, I said to my kid, "Hey, do you want to go to the airport and watch the planes taking off?"

"Yeah!"

"Good. Let's go."

As he was doomed to be a lonely attacker, I asked him if he liked Mahmoud's style of coaching.

"What coaching?" he asked.

As we watched the big birds roar down the runway, I thought about the upcoming game against the team from the barrio. Jet fuel filled my lungs.

THE SPORTING GREEN

TEN–NIL

The Dragons scored a goal on Saturday and it was a classic. Manny, the Dragons' sweeper, belted the ball into the roof of the Dragons' net, an own goal. The goalie, Drake, spent the game either rooted to the spot or diving in the wrong direction after the ball had hit the back of the net. Not that he was to blame entirely for the other nine goals scored by Local Cruz Azul, a fine squad of young Latino

soccer talent, content to show no mercy to their more afflu-
ent peers.

Within minutes of the kickoff, the Latino magicians had
cast a spell of paralysis on the bunch of yellow bananas.
Coach Mahmoud spluttered under his breath in suppressed
Farsi while parents bleated useless calls of encouragement.
The Dragons' defense resembled Swiss cheese or, if you
are lactose- but not latex-intolerant, a breached condom.
But as the *Sporting Green* is a family newspaper we must
keep the references to sex to a minimum. Suffice to say, the
Dragons' performance on Saturday was about as much fun
as a dose of syphilitic gonorrhea.

A happy ambivalence settled on the team at halftime,
as they devoured the organic produce and asked their parents if they could play baseball instead. In the second half,
Assistant Coach Black could be seen with his hands at his
throat, although it was difficult to tell if he was choking on
a monkey nut and in need of the Heimlich maneuver or if it
was a warning to the defenders that a noose was waiting
for them at the end of the game. A Cruz Azul player taunted
Jonathan, the Dragons' left back, who in turn told his mum,
who in turn instructed Coach Black to bring the matter up
with the referee at the end of the game. The referee asked
the Dragon what the opposing player had said to him. "He
said I sucked," was the reply. Coach Black shrugged his
shoulders and said, "Fair enough." Jonathan's mum was
furious at Coach Black's agreement, prompting speculation
that difficult days may lie ahead for the Scottish coach when
it comes to keeping out of the dock of the parents' court.

At the postgame press conference Coach Black blamed
the players and the parents. "Soccer is not a sport for soft-

ies," he said, "and it pains me to say that the moms and dads are encouraging such behavior. I have thereby instructed the parents to remove all comfort from their children's lives: pillows and soft toys and security blankets. We must toughen up and learn to fight. No more watching *Dragon Tales*. It's *Rambo* and *Terminator* for these boys now. They are to spend their waking hours learning from true American heroes. Chuck Norris, for example. I trust I have the parents' full backing."

CHAPTER 5

Strictly Speaking

Discipline. No campaign, be it sporting or otherwise, could be successful without it. And I knew all about discipline.

I had the word belted into me as a kid in Scotland. Discipline in our schools was applied to the student body via the end of a leather belt, known as a *tawse*.

A company whose owner was called John Dick manufactured tawses. The weapon was twenty-two inches long, made from the flexible but firm ass-cheeks of a bull, and featured a split thong. Its sole purpose on the planet was to do severe damage to schoolchildren. The maximum times a schoolteacher could brutalize a student in a single attack was six.

"Out for the belt!" was a cry when a poor kid was caught displaying a lack of discipline.

Marched to the front of the room, the student would face the class.

"Hands up!" the teacher screeched.

Any educator worth his salt knew, too, that if he made the student raise the sleeve on his shirt, collateral damage could be done to the wrist. The cuff turned back, the adult in the room, enraged as he was with muscle and authority, would bring the belt down on the hand of the child. The noise was sickening, beef on mitt. The rest of the class winced. The victim usually doubled over in agony; once in a while the child would actually collapse, only to be told to get back on his or her feet for another assault.

"Six of the best!" they called it. The best.

The humiliation in front of the class only added to the suffering. You didn't cry—that would be fatal to one's reputation. Rebel kids wore the number of beltings they had received like a badge of glory.

The echo of the blow finally gone, all that was left was silence.

Imagine having to pick up a pencil after that. Fortunately, the lesson itself was fucked up completely by the violence. Kids couldn't concentrate.

One teacher in particular, a man called Mr. McLean who taught Classics and Latin, had a particularly gruesome love of the tawse, even giving it a name (Ebeneezer). He recited a little poem before delivering the beating. McLean liked to hit kids when they couldn't parse the ablative case.

"Ebeneezer, big and black, give this child a nasty whack," McLean would sing.

Thwack! The air would be sucked out the room, the blood sucked out of the skin.

One time, I heard belting sounds coming from the adjacent changing room after a school soccer game. We had just delivered a huge defeat to a visiting team. Their coach must have decided the loss merited a round of beltings. Maybe the defenders were whacked for their lack of concentration at corner kicks, or the midfield for its poor tackling, or the attackers for their missed open goals—all good enough reasons for violence.

But what was worse—a tawse to the hand or a tongue-lashing? I had given the Dragons one at the last practice. Told them to shut up. I had said "friggin." At least I had not said "fucking," but my tongue would have to be lashed to the mast. Once a careless word left the deck, the damage could be extensive.

"What are you? A fern or a soccer player?"

Comments like that could prove fatal, especially when you looked at the specimen who had fathered our foliage.

The Fern's daddy was built tough, like his automobile. Rippled, he displayed an undulating landscape of unblemished skin, taut fresh flesh just about keeping back bulging muscles. He was one helluva sandwich. His arms looked like they had been reared on cans of spinach. I imagined his reaction to my mind's abuse of his son:

"You called my son a fern! You Scottish bastard!" At this, I would start to run, and would probably never stop.

I would never be a true American macho man. Scottish men rarely grew chest muscles. As a wee laddie, I was around guys who preferred hanging their physiques on Quasimodostyle spinal curvatures, tobacco-thrashed chests, and flabby skin that hung down like dingleberries. No amount of exercise, implants, or surgery could eradicate an entire genealogy of poor posture; no Alexander Technique could overcome the hunched shoulders of the northern Scot. Up in the freezing rainy parts of the planet, where long dark winter months hung blackness on folks, hunching up to protect oneself from the biting elements was the only possible pose. Our bodies were flowers, expanding in light, shrinking in darkness. Most of my days, there was barely any sunlight.

The Fern's dad muscled over to me after practice, expecting something like conversation I guess. It was everything I could do to not say, "Does he have a lot of potted plants in his room at home, by any chance?" Instead, out loud I said, "Your boy is one of the best players on the team and it is a real pleasure to be coaching him."

As I spoke, I felt my curvature arch over by one more degree, as the bind of a lie tightened around my watery spine.

• • • •

My patience with the Dragons was beginning to stretch like a fraying rubber band. Two games and we had conceded twenty-two goals and never had the ball in the opponent's half of the field. I might not have had the solid frame, but I could say that I was no quitter. Hope must prevail. I had not moved to these suburbs to put up shutters, to skulk in the darkness of my mind. I needed to be at the center of things, shake hands with my suburban fellows, set a paternal example, and deliver victory to the Dragons, at all costs. If I didn't remind myself of this I would get Alzheimer's and lose my keys to the future.

It was three a.m.—time to raid the new fridge. My city-living eating had rarely been done in the apartment. Suburban chow, on the other hand, was done at home at the kitchen table with the family. The marvel of the new skyscraper refrigerator impressed me. It was prime chilled real estate, featuring six shelves and six drawers. I could have adopted a family of starving pygmies and housed them in it—I could even charge them rent to help pay my mortgage. The produce vaults contained multicolored fresh organic vegetables. Other drawers were packed with meat from cows that had had better diets than homeless people, and gallons of milk and jugs of juice sat like small buildings on a glass-covered terrace. In the polar regions of the fridge, fish waited to be warmed up and Ben and Jerry sat freezing their balls off. It was the grandness of the American refrigerator that had seduced me when I first set foot on these shores. My boyhood Scottish refrigerator was so tiny a midget would never have found a bed in it.

I grabbed Ben and Jerry from the freezer and spoke to them.

"Things suck here with this soccer team. The players are multiple flavors, frozen rigid, no warmth. They're like a tub of your bloody rainbow ice cream."

Ben looked at Jerry. Jerry looked at Ben.

I pulled the lid off and the cows of Vermont mooed.

I was just in time to catch the last letter of the night from the faithful to Reverend Murray. I couldn't quite make out the question as the sound warbled and the sync went haywire, but I imagined that a follower asked whether or not mail got delivered in heaven. Ben and Jerry melted as my eyes turned to Nod.

CHAPTER 6

Multicultural Nuts

After the drubbing by the sons of Central America in the last game, I decided to think about the difference between their team and ours. The working-class barrio team was, simply put, homogenous: Every player was from the same national root. They knew the menu. Their halftime snack was a healthy tortilla wrap and a few chips. Solid nosh. We had pita and hummus, French water, and those damned exotic world snacks that were unidentifiable and seemed loaded with explosive indigestive danger, something that would be laid out at a United Nations banquet. Their vocal instructions were unified and clear, too. No one missed the call when the coaches fired in a message from the sidelines. By contrast, translators and subtitles were needed for the Dragons as the Scottish and Iranian barks drifted upward to be lost in the rays of a bright and burning sun. No one understood my cries of *Loada shite* and *Fer fuck sake*. Who understood the mumbling Farsi curses Mahmoud was offloading? The parent voices on the sidelines added to the confusion.

We emitted West Indian shrieks, Kurdish cracks, white collegiate yippees, and shattering shrills from the queens of Soccermomland.

Was it possible to harmonize paprika and haggis, melt yogurt with beans, fry kebabs in lard, and dump ackee and salt fish in a bowl of hot Kurdish dowjic? America prided itself on its blending belief. Put enough grind into the dream and soon enough America's immigrants would have taste buds not for home but for homes, consumption, and flag waving. If I could just get my hands on one of those power blenders that caused hearing loss among employees at the juice joint in the mall, I could dump in the Dragons and make a winning smoothie.

And on the religious front, we were ecumenical disunity at its most American. The whole Latino squad had crossed themselves and said their prayers in Spanish as they hit the soccer field. They were Pope fans to a man. To accommodate the Dragons' faiths, on the other hand, we would need prayer mat deliveries from the Middle East, bricklayers building Western walls, Rastafarian bud and Bibles, holy stone blocks from Azteca, and chilly Scottish Protestants delivering ass-freezing pews from gloomy churches in darkest Scotland. Rainbow coalitions might have worked for political votes and assembling the varied choices of gay San Francisco, but could it work in coaching a multicultural kids' soccer team in the suburbs?

What we needed was a government pamphlet.

U.S. GOVERNMENT INFORMATION GUIDE

How to Defuse Conflict in a Multicultural America

Our great country has passed through many changes. Where once the white man ruled over the land, the new America is a face made up of all human stripes. To ensure that our nation's fabric remains strong, this pamphlet is designed to give you some tips on how to live in a multicultural society.

Pay attention to notices in the media about upcoming cultural events, gatherings like ethnic food festivals, visiting foreign dance troupes, or touring bands from places like Africa. Take your family and experience the joy of the world's cultural menu. From vindaloo curry to hot chili peppers, from spicy Cajun soups to haggis, let your taste buds loose. And partake in the religious freedoms of other cultures. Christians can send a Muslim a greeting during Ramadan. Muslims can light a candle on a menorah. Jews can wear a Santa hat. Whatever it is, make it known that you are a part of the lives of others.

Offense and conflict are inevitable in any society, but they can be prevented from becoming prejudice and hate.

When you feel that you have trampled all over the sensitivity of others, step back carefully and swish away the dirt like a baseball umpire at home plate. Look closely at the person you have just trodden on. Time is of the essence. Don't delay. Always carry a small dictionary of friendly ethnic apologies that can be used to disarm the insulted. Without such a timely apology, you run the risk of not being a good neighbor.

And no one wants this to happen. Neighborliness is the heart and soul of America. Welcoming immigrants to our land is part of our pursuit of happiness and low wages.

Enjoy your meal, and have a nice day.

I knew of what I thought. When people called me English I went berserk, erupting with a boom of unpleasant tartan adjectives. I had grown up saying *Fuck the English*, as if they were all part of some abstract blame for bad weather and no jobs. Here in the Bay Area, political correctness was an absolute. The place demanded it. If I were going to run for mayor, I would need to nail this stuff down, and quick. I needed to be more like those masters of political correctness, the ones who always got 100 percent on school tests and who, once grown, rarely got belted or offended anyone.

In the language control department, I was at a disadvantage due to my national background and occupation. Swearing was a hobby for many Scottish people—the English had their gardens, we had fuck and shit and piss and wanker. And I had worked in bars my whole life, and they tended to be places rife with inventive cussing. I swore too much, I fucking knew that. But I wasn't the only one to blame, and it wasn't just swearing. At work, my ears were exposed to drunken twenty-something speech, which to my mind was worse than imprecations. Like, whatever, so totally—what the fuck had happened to us? *You know, it's, like, so totally rad, but, like, whatever!* Simile speech fever had taken over a whole generation's language structure. "Fucking" was the least of our worries. I knew I could avoid that in front of the team, but "like"? I vowed to stick to metaphor.

"Manny, your kick is so, like, whatever! You're a mule!"

To feel relaxed in the multicultural world, it was vital to mix socially with people from all walks of life. My neighbor, for example, was Cuban. From my kitchen window, I could see his TV was the size of a small planet. Soccer or baseball was on twenty-three hours a day, the other hour being filled by porn. When he had a party, music swelled, sexy women danced, and men with beards who looked like a branch of the Fidel Castro Supporters Club stood on the porch smoking cigars. I went over to practice my election handshake, raise an elbow, and talk sports to real fanatics. A small goal had been set up in the side yard, next to a table filled with snacks and beer. Some of the Castroans were whacking a soccer ball into the empty net.

"Hey, it looks like you comrades could do with a goalkeeper!" I said. "I'll do it."

Sadly, a day of drinking had given them each mule-like shots, and they took great pleasure in using my head as a target. Balls hit me like I was at a paintball convention, and beer bottles were knocked all over the place.

"Hey, my name's not Miami!" I cried, rubbing my bruises. I gave up on the goalkeeping and grabbed a beer. As we chatted, I explained to the Cubans the stresses of coaching the Dragons.

"Your team will never win," said a man in green fatigues after hearing my anxieties surrounding the Dragons' composition. "Too many tastes. The revolution is always one color, my friend. It sounds like you need some direct intervention. How many goals did you say you had lost in two games? You need to invent a god, amigo."

We didn't need to. We already had one. Without showing any disrespect to the magnificence of the Aztec culture or to the tongue-twisting fatigue in pronouncing the names of their deities, the Dragons' central midfielder was blessed with a name that sounded like Zalopotechx.

"Can I call him Zalo?" I asked his hippie mother, hoping that she had heard of the soccer legend Edison Arantes do Nascimento, who wisely went by a *nom de football*, Pelé.

"No! He's named after an Aztec god!" she snarled. And she was right. People should have been able to run "Zalohopatecaxul," although I couldn't be sure that was it, either, off their tongues like a BBC World Service announcer spreading Oxbridge effluvium over the obstacles of nomenclature. My mouth was not butter. Clunked and fixed as it was by names like Smith and Jones, Jim and Mary, the Aztec pantheon of gods fitted like cheap dentures in my dodgy Scottish mouth.

She stressed the eight-syllable deity name to Mahmoud

and myself but we were monotheists used to three- and five-letter derivatives of Immanence. It was not going to work.

"Just listen!" she demanded.

Zaloahectical seemed depressed. He cried a lot, even while playing soccer. He puffed and chased the ball but it was a fruitless search through endless teardrops. His bizarre flower-power haircut was laden down with colored beads that sounded like a wind chime. Just walking must have driven him to madness with the clatter of beads. I could see the future when the God of Vengeance and Retribution would take over and Mummy would pay, and not just for the hearing aid. He had no friends; his teammates did not know what to call him; no nickname was allowed, no abbreviation for an Aztec god.

"Try and kick the ball," I yelled at Zalonohelpatall, although this time I was sure. He just stopped dead in his tracks and wept.

"How many weird nuts are on this fucking team?" I asked no one in particular. No one answered.

CHAPTER 7

On the Offensive with the Tribe

The sport of soccer likely started when a decapitated head rolled along a battlefield and was booted by some pissed-off medieval grunt. (Some would argue that English fans keep that history alive with their hooliganism.) The Scottish actually lay claim to being the inventor of soccer. The ancient Roman Empire had come to our country with hopes of opening pasta restaurants and pizzerias, but a few days after they arrived the local population ate them, burped, and kept their indigestible Italian heads for a kick about.

Word soon spread back to Rome that they might be better avoiding such hazardous places. So they sent construction teams instead to the edge of the empire and built a big wall—Hadrian's—to keep the Scottish tribes away from civilization. It had a profound effect on the development of Scottish thinking and cemented the power of tribes, or clans, as they came to be known.

Glasgow, my hometown, has the most virulent soccer tribal rivalry in the world. My city of three-quarters of a million people has three huge soccer stadiums: one for the Catholics, one for the Protestants, and one for the rest.

The two main rival branches, though, are the world-famous Glasgow Rangers and the world-famous Glasgow Celtic, or together, "the Old Firm." Their totems are sunk deep into the history of the country. Celtic fans paint themselves with the colors of immigrant Irish Catholic green, with the Pope's head at the top; the Rangers fans sport deep Scottish Protestant blue, and frame a portrait of Her Majesty, Queen Elizabeth II, in their parlors, proud they are that Scotland is part of the Protestant United Kingdom.

On Saturdays, during the soccer season, tens of thousands of the tribesmen gather in their cathedral-like stadiums to worship their creeds and their teams with rousing songs of battle and blood. Rangers fans sing, *We're up to our knees in Fenian* [Catholic] *blood,* while Celtic's Catholics chant, *To die an Orange* [Protestant] *bastard is a horrible way to go.* No wonder, then, that some followers are so pumped full of hatred that they contemplate murder. The atmosphere during games between the two teams is unmatched anywhere—the loathing is palpable. The mass aggression makes you sweat in buckets. After the game, you leave the stadium lighter, pounds gone through fear.

The police operation alone is a major security exercise, featuring hundreds of cops, riot police, horses, armored vehicles, shields, batons, rubber bullets, tear gas, you name it. The emergency rooms at hospitals load up on extra bandages and splints; surgeons keep their hands clean and wait anxiously for the gurneys to arrive, stocked as they will be with slashed skin and mashed heads. Amazingly, doctors know to keep green and blue scrubs on hand, as some arrivals at the emergency room only allow themselves to be treated if the doctor is wearing the colors of their team.

Sane people, on the other hand, know to stay home on match days. Dogs bark as if there are fireworks outside.

The power of the tribes doesn't just make itself known in the soccer stadiums—it also makes its way into the public schools in the city, which are segregated between Catholics and Protestants, with other ethnic and religious minorities usually tossed in with the latter. Protestant kids sing, *Fuck the Pope*. Catholic kids sing, *Fuck the Queen*.

Prejudice, sectarianism, and bigotry were the three main values I grew up around, all manifested in a game in which twenty-two men run around after a white piece of air-filled leather.

It wasn't just abstract, either—it was personal. One day when I was still a teenager, a gang of thugs ambushed me, as I returned late at night from a friend's house.

"We're going to rip your face," one said.

"Hold on," said another. "Are you a Proddie [Protestant] or a Tim [Catholic]?"

It was the six-million-dollar question in Glasgow. Answer wrongly and your mum would be getting her sewing kit out to stitch your face back together.

I noticed the freckles on one of the assailants. I hoped it meant he was of Catholic Irish ancestry.

"I'm for the Pope," I said, and home I went, beauty preserved. Other victims when asked the same question, and without the guidance of freckles, pleaded, "Jewish," but this was always met with the bad Glasgow joke,

"Aye. Is that a Catholic Jew or a Protestant Jew?"

None of this madness could ever happen in modern multicultural America, of course. The idea of being fanatically attached to a color, to be willing to commit acts of horror against others of a different sporting stripe, was beyond preposterous. The closest Americans got to tribal behavior in sports was drunken Raiders fans bonking 49ers fans over the head with jumbo hot dogs at tailgate parties. As for Major League Soccer . . . well, I saw a video on YouTube once of a bunch of DC fans "fighting" with New Yorkers. It looked like a tea party.

One thing was for sure. Defeated tribes are racked with trauma. I know all about trauma.

For a start, I was once shot playing soccer.

* * * *

It had started out like any other day late in the Scottish year. The last embers of auburn smoldered in the late autumnal trees, but besides that, it was fucking cold. My team was having a practice session. We wore nothing save our paper-thin soccer strips, and our arms and legs were blue. Snot was running like rivers into our mouths and jamming our teeth. The effort of sprinting in this weather popped our faces beetroot.

It was fucking marvelous.

Then it happened. At first I thought it was a joke. Three older kids, masked and wrapped in blankets of blue scarves, walked onto the field and grabbed our goalkeeper by the neck. Time slowed; what we thought was a joke quickly turned horribly hostile. One of the assailants had a gun pointed at our goalie's head. A gun, I said. Autumn turned to deepest winter. We were eleven years old.

We thought we were going to die.

The other two kids also drew guns. Now not only the goalkeeper but my brother, too, was being held at gunpoint. The third kid rounded up the rest of us.

"Who's in fucking charge here?" one of the gunmen demanded.

Everyone looked at me.

The guy holding a gun to my brother picked up the ball and threw it at me. It bounced off my leg and rolled back to him.

"Listen," he said, "I'm going to kick the ball and you are going to run and get it and bring it back like a fucking dog. And if you don't, your pals will get shot."

With that, he took a huge swipe and the ball raced down the field. I chased it, of course, wishing only that I could fly off the end of the world. When I brought the ball back, he immediately kicked it off into the distance once more. Most of my players were now holding back the sobs. Knees knocked in the freeze. There were no adults around to save us. We were in this on our own.

Boot. The ball raced away again. I lost count, that day, of

how many times I ran to fetch it. But it couldn't go on; I had to do something.

I had one shot, literally. And it had to be my fiercest ever, a deadly accurate bullet that would hit this evil bastard square in the face. As I returned once more, the three bandits were laughing and joking with each other, their attention wandering. I saw my chance. I picked up the ball, dropped it in front of me, and fired a blistering half-volley that scorched the air and hit the first gunman smack in the chest.

"Run!" I yelled at my players, turning to do the same myself.

The team split, screaming as they ran. My brother, though, was still at gunpoint, and I turned back to see if he was okay. What I saw horrified me—one of my friends was being held down as the gunmen fired into his leg at close range. This scared me even more, and then, well, then I was hit in the chest, and then the side of my head.

I've never run so fast in all my life. I didn't care that I was bleeding. In fact, I ran all the way home, at least a couple of city blocks. My mum was horrified, and called both police and doctor immediately. Amazingly, the doctor arrived first, and pronounced me fine, as though he knew what he was talking about. A few minutes after he left, the police arrived and performed a desultory interview, the only remarkable part of which was the revelation that the gun had in fact been firing pellets, not bullets.

I wondered how they knew, given that they told us they'd never get the gunmen. At age eleven, guns were what you saw on *Kojak* or *Starsky and Hutch,* not in a field in Glasgow. So it didn't matter that it had "only" been a BB gun. All of us had thought the weapons were real. It was only later, when others laughed at us for thinking they were loaded with real bullets, that we played down the assault and laughed it off. The scars from the pellets hung around a while, long enough for me to develop a lust for revenge.

●　●　●　●

It would be unwise of me to actually shoot any of the players in Dragonland, of course, but several parents had surely noticed my increasing use of strangulation gestures. After one particularly difficult practice, one of them, who I reckoned was a doctor, came over to me.

"Can I corral your ear?" said Dr. John.

I was nervous. I imagined him with a lasso chasing after me on the field, roping my neck and hog-tying legs and arms. Instead, Dr. John stepped forward and leaned in close.

"The message is too negative. You need to have an alternative strategy, and you and Mahmoud need to embrace offense as an ideal motivator."

"Mahmoud's in charge of the offense," I said, defensively.

"No, I don't mean it in those terms. I mean it as an overall strategy. The kids are unhappy with losing by big scores. We need to constantly be on the offense when it comes to message. It's a value the kids need to hear. Positive reinforcement."

"You're absolutely right," I said obediently, and in a posh, polite voice.

Dr. John's game was psychiatry, the hanging judge of medicine. He had analyzed my personality and coaching message and condemned it. His eye had witnessed my twitching body movements as I aped up and down the line, failing to hold back my violent strangling gesticulations, uncontrolled suppressed oaths, and involuntary deep knee bends.

I could tell he thought I had ODD, oppositional defiant disorder, which, according to the *DSM,* the psychiatrist's bible, is a "recurrent pattern of negativistic, defiant, disobedient, and hostile behavior."

You got it, Dr. John! That ODD guy with the weird fucking accent, right on! I knew you admired me, I knew you were all jealous of my tones; you were stuck with your bland American drawls, an accent that everyone in the world hated! My accent had been enough to get me laid! People thought I was James Bond!

But Dr. John's offensive prescription was not to be ignored. I never ignored a doctor. The first dose of offense was administered right before game 3.

The Dragons were gathering to have their team photograph taken, a tradition in every sport. Photographs in this style adorned the halls of sporting history, from mantelpieces to sports bars. Fingerprints smudged the glass as fans pointed to the faces of heroes. Remember her run, remember his strike, and remember his goal.

I hesitated. I was feeling a pulse of loathing. I thought I would give the snap a bye. Mahmoud was angered by my desire not to have my photograph taken with the Dragons.

"It might damage my run for office if I show up in it," I said jokingly.

"Get in the picture!" yelled Mahmoud.

Dr. John's offensive pill had worked.

Grudgingly, I obeyed. I speculated that Mahmoud's motive to have me included was for insurance purposes. In the future he could point to me and say, "That Scottish asshole was to blame for the worst team in sporting history."

I stepped to the back row of the squad and squinted.

"Look forward. Smile, boys," said the photographer.

The blunt and unhappy smiles of two foreign men ruined the American picture.

The game itself kicked off under a heavy, moody cloud on this otherwise bright and sunny day. Predictably, by halftime the Dragons had collected a heavy bag of conceded goals.

"Well played, everyone. You guys are great. We'll get the ten goals back in the second half. You should be proud of yourselves."

I made sure Dr. John heard my optimism.

As I chewed on my halftime organic Granny Smith, a mealymouthed messenger from our opponents took the long journey down the sideline, behind the goal, round the corner flag, and into our territory. He asked to sequester Mahmoud's and my ear.

"We'll lay off you in the second half, give you guys a chance to get a goal, so as the kids don't feel overwhelmed."

"F-f-f—," I stuttered, trying to hold back the inevitable

curse. But it was no use. "Fucking charity! You must be joking. No way! What an insult!"

I spent the second half screaming, pleading, urging, bursting, cursing, beckoning, straining, bending, strutting, and farting Granny Smith. Then, as if by magic, Manny managed to kick the ball, like a fucking mule, into the opponents' half, sending the Dragons charging down the field in a mad stampede. The ball bobbled close to the enemy goal—it was a chance, our first chance of the season—and Mahmoud's son, the striker, went for it. Mahmoud and I held our breaths, a glimpse of paradise, quiet, rich, virgins everywhere, and the play moved in slow motion and spread its wings across our desperate hopes. The ball was there, right there in front of the goal, and he raised his leg to kick and . . . missed it completely.

Laughter erupted from the opponents' side of the field. I was going to kill someone. It was time to use eggs Benedict headlines on these charity-offering bastards. One of them over there was going to get worked over easy at the end of the game.

Mahmoud saw my switch flip.

"No," he said.

Keeping track of the number of goals in the second half that sank the Dragons into a mine from which they would never again see the light of day was pointless. Parents complained that the league should have a policy limiting the number of goals a team could score. No one had seen a team as bad as the Dragons before. No team had conceded goals by the baker's dozen.

THE SPORTING GREEN

SHOOT THAT POISON ARROW

You have to travel back in time to the Battle of Agincourt, 1415, to find the meaning of flipping the bird, Assistant Coach Black's disgraceful act toward the opponents at the end of Saturday's debacle. On the medieval battlefield, English archers gave the middle finger to their French enemies, and then proceeded to slaughter them with their longbow arrows resplendent with the feathers of plucked pheasant in the fletching. Thus giving the bird.

There were plenty of poison arrows on display at Saturday's Dragons game. Number one in the quiver was Coach Black's vulgarity. The family values limitations observed by this newspaper prevent a verbatim recollection of Black's verbal abuse. The atmosphere he created was hardly indicative of plucking a pheasant—"*ucking unpleasant" would be more accurate.

With the defeat adding to the feeling that the Dragons' season is an elevator severed from its cable, the atmosphere is understandably strained, but nothing can justify an inflammatory crude gesture when children are present.

At the postmatch press conference, Coach Black was asked about his offensive digit.

"Well, it's the Digital Age, after all. I guess I could have sent their coach an e-mail complaining about his insulting offer to stop scoring goals against us. Is that not the ultimate in condescension? So I flipped him off. It's the fastest instant message. And now that you members of the press are so intent on pursuing the matter, let me give you vultures a bonus middle digit on the other hand. Now you get the message."

Maybe he should take a look in the mirror. Saturday's team performance provided enough conclusive evidence that no coaching is taking place for the Dragons. The simple ideas behind organizing a soccer team are non-existent. Kids need to be taught. Someone needs to buy a blackboard to show the players where to stand and how to move in relation to the ball. Why are the defenders, Coach Black's charges, unable to move up the field with the ball? Why are they standing still around the penalty box when the ball is momentarily in the opponents' half?

Rumblings are rising among the Dragons fans. Long dark parcels of penetrating glares are flying toward Coach Mahmoud and the Scot. And the packaging is marked in big black letters spelling the word that all coaches fear, LOSER. Once that label sticks to the surface, no amount of effort can strip it off. Neither rain nor hail nor sleet nor snow will stop the mailman from putting that toxic parcel in their hands.

CHAPTER 8

Who Are You?

Dear Reverend Murray,

I work in a place of sin. I stay awake at night to catch the Bible study as I have to cleanse myself of the grog stains that I give to others. I confess to giving people with large livers larger livers. I have put more people in the grave than some of the bad guys in the Holy Book. But I am not writing you to ask for forgiveness, for only God can clean the bar of dregs, but I do want to know if it is okay to cuss the thing that makes you take the Lord's name in vain. I know this question sounds as if it might have been written by one of those damn intellexuals but be assured that I try to keep my exuals straight.

When I shout, "Jesus Christ" it is in anger at the losing soccer team that I coach. We have lost three games in a row by a number of goals that add up to the age of Noah when he died. Can you pray for my team, please? And for me! I'm taking the Lord's name in vain! I'm weak! I cuss! I confess! We need all the help we can get.

Some of our opponents are Catholics from Mexico

*and I know that they are heretics but I know that men-
tioning that on the air will bring you problems just like it
did when they said that you didn't like black people even
though you might tap your foot to "Thriller" by Mike
Jackson if you hear it on the radio.*

> *Yours faithfully,*
> *Alan Black*

The concept of the "wee man" in Scotland holds a special place in the culture. The "wee man" is admired, not looked down upon like Napoleon and his complex. It is not uncommon to see Scottish men sitting on booster seats in restaurants. Platform shoes do a surprisingly brisk trade. The little guys do their best to be photographed on hills and the like. It all comes down, literally, to a lack of vegetables in the diet; that, and limited sunlight.

The concept of the "wee man" can only exist if there are "big men," of course, and I reside in this smaller though bigger division. I grew because my mum gave me brussels sprouts once a year.

This size dichotomy has led to manifold episodes of pugilistic engagement, of course—it being Scotland, the "wee man" often assaults the "big man" for no other reason than that he's taller. I always hated it when a "wee man" flew through the air to clock a "big man" on the chin. Often it was only because the diminutive's friends had goaded him into it, urging him to claim a prize scalp from a man that much higher in the atmosphere.

It happened to me one day in elementary school. A kid the size of a regular garden gnome took a running leap, swung his tiny fist, and clocked me on my left ear. There was nothing I could do, so I looked down at the wee fellow, put my hand on the top of his head, brought my knee up sharply, and stopped his smirk with a strong blow to the chin. He would have spat out teeth for days if he'd had any to speak of (or speak through for that matter).

We had a wee man on the Dragons, but I never wanted to knee him in the face. I called him Speedy Gonzalez. He sped across the blades of grass like ten to the power of ten. Turning right, then spinning left, whips on his heels, flying backward, jumping forward, round and round and over he went. He was buzzing like the "Flight of the Bumblebee." When he stopped running, his hands played his chest like Van Cliburn with a ferret up his butt. Speedy was a Ritalin candidate.

"You're Speedy Gonzalez. *Arriba! Arriba! Ándale!*" I yelled in admiration and encouragement. "Go on, Speedy Gonzalez! Get the ball! Take it up the field!"

I was amazed at how this tiny fleck of child could vroom so fast. If only he could be taught to run with the ball toward the correct goal we might be able to score. I took him aside at a training session for big man to wee man management.

"Speedy Gonzalez, you're our magic mouse, wee man. Keep eating the cheese. Here's what I want you to do with the ball."

"Dad!" he yelled.

"Speedy Gonzalez? What's that?" said his dad, somewhat of a dwarf with hair that resembled barbed wire. Mahmoud had told me that Speedy's father was a Kurd. His fused eyebrows glared up at me from down below as I attempted to take the Mexican cartoon comparison to Kurdistan, all with a Scottish accent.

"Mexico! No, no, no!" Dad protested. It was not a label he wanted his sire to be confused with. He seemed offended. Apparently, viewers in Kurdistan had never fiddled with a TV aerial on Saturday morning searching for Warner Brothers cartoons. If I had known a Kurd would balk at a Mexican stereotype I would have reached for my Kurdish dictionary, and replaced *Arriba! Arriba!* with *Xera! Xera!* Somewhere in Kurdish history there had to be a speedy rodent but my subsequent Internet search for a Kurdish metaphor proved fruitless. A mountain people, they had little connection to a culture of mass acceleration, although they had produced a tiny soccer player who flew around the field as if he was on a magic carpet.

"Where are you from?" he asked in a strange voice.

"Scotland."

"I don't know it," he said.

"You've not seen *Braveheart*? I thought everyone had."

●　●　●　●

But what did folks in America really think when the word "Scotland" arose?

Was it a country where men wore thick plaid skirts and no

underwear and liked to listen to a windy musical pipe that blared laments for the fallen? Had folks heard of the haggis they ate there, that sheep's stomach dish, filled with a diabolical mush of ground-up body parts layered in a moss of inedible oatmeal? Did they think of golf and how Scotland is the birthplace of that mindless game of small balls and tailored slacks to which they felt such religious devotion? Or did they drink Scotland, before and after dinner, single malts and blends to set the heart afire?

No. Mostly they thought of Mel Gibson, Scotland's greatest Australian, the man who single-handedly put the trials of the nation on the map with that fucking movie about a man considered the founder of the concept that America loved most. (Freedom.)

Some knew more, though. In the Deep South, people recognized Scotland for its place in their ancestral roots, and for its influence in the lore of the Confederacy. Take a peek at Scotland's flag, the Cross of St. Andrew, then compare it to the Battle Flag of Dixie. Or how about the Klan? It's not called the Klan for nothing, founded as it was by Scots after the Civil War. Burning crosses? See under Glasgow Rangers and Glasgow Celtic.

But in California I lost track of how many times I had heard the following comments:

"I just love your accent."

"What's under your kilt?" (Oh, how I wanted to answer, "My fucking hairy balls.")

"Do you believe in the Loch Ness Monster?"

But the brogue my mouth couldn't hide would mitigate any answer.

"Awright, boays! Geez yer ears fer a minute. Noo listen tay me! Ur we gonnay win the day?" I yelled at the team.

"What?" said Manny.

"Are . . . we . . . going . . . to . . . win . . . today?"

"No."

"Of course we are! Look at them. They're rubbish."

"You said we were rubbish."

"No, we're good against them. Come on. Let's win today. Let's see how it feels to score a goal. Let's give Drake here a break."

"I don't need a break," said our goalie. "I don't want to play goalie no more."

"You have to, you're our goalie."

A finger poked me in the back.

"He doesn't want to be goalie, mon," said his dad, the Rastafarian, or at least the man with the Rastafarian haircut.

"He gets no help from the defenders. He is no longer the goalie. He will play in the outfield. The players need to be rotated in different positions. It's obviously not working."

How perceptive, I thought. He had unilaterally decided this team change without counsel to the Scottish and Iranian pashas. I would have to shoot him down in a council with Mahmoud, but if Mahmoud agreed with the Rastafarian's request, I'd have to shoot him, too, and then deny it in a song.

"I'll bring it up with Mahmoud," I said.

The prematch intelligence on today's opponents was good. There was hope. Made from the same blended parts of multicultural suburbia, today's enemy likely possessed the same level of player that wore the colors of the Dragons. I checked them out. Several of them were wearing glasses.

"Look at them. We're playing against a school for the blind. Come on, Dragons! This is our chance. Are we going to let a bunch of wee speckies beat us? Who are ya?"

"The Dragons!"

The opponents' parents were no doubt as committed to the principle of childhood happiness as we were over in the land of Dragons. On the other side of the field I could see their soccer moms, enamel on display, sparkle smiles and ponytails. Dads in baseball caps and free from shaving for a day stood with arms folded and sporting personas on full beam. Coffee cups welded to hands, chatter bubbly like champagne. The Dragons' parents stood glumly looking at the ground waiting for it to shake with another seismic loss.

Game 4 kicked off. The Dolt in Need of a Volt was our new goalie. His battery needed the cables, the sky was blue again, and the referee was a wanker, and bald. Within two minutes he was castigating Dragons for infractions against the throw-in rule.

"Oh, come on, Ref," I yelled.

The man in the middle ignored me. A few minutes later,

he blew for a foul against Speedy Gonzalez, who had crashed into an opponent.

"Fer fuck sake, Ref. That's not a foul. That wee specky fell over his own two feet. He's blind."

And when our Aztec god was clipped from behind and sent tumbling, the referee ignored the entire thing.

"Come on, baldy! That's a foul! You're blind, too—why don't you borrow a pair of specs from the favored team? What is this, a gathering of the sensory impaired?"

Finally, the chrome dome's radar screen picked up my blip of taunts. His striped yellow top went off like a flare. He ran toward me, behind the enemy goal, where I had been niggling their goalie with a low-voiced critique.

Now the referee was foaming at the mouth, right in my face.

"That's against the law," he said.

"Am I under arrest?"

"You know what I mean. I'll report you to the league and you will be banned from coaching."

As he ran off, I turned up the volume,

"You'll be doing me a favor, pal. But let me ask you this. How about I contact the league and tell them that you are turning your blind eyes to bad tackles against my team and it is going to result in injuries and lawsuits against you and the league? And what if I tell all the parents that you are bi-ased and offensive and a danger to the welfare of children? I bet you don't have kids. Why are you here? Now, I'll shut up if you show some fairness. That's right. You got it. Jog on."

His yellow top looked more like a big yellow stripe down his fat sweaty back.

I continued the baiting of their goalie.

"You'll never make it as a goalie. You're too wee. The ball is going to go straight through your legs."

He turned and looked at me. His eyes bugged out from behind his glasses, like supersize saucers, as if alien spaceships had landed on his sockets. My work here was done.

As I returned to my position next to our supreme leader, Mahmoud, cheers erupted from the other side of the field. We were one–nil down. The collective head of the Dragon sank, the eye of the Dragon closed, the ears withered, and the tail went limp.

"Come on!" I yelled. "Fight back. Remember to fight back! We're Dragons. Fight back and claw!"

Mahmoud was facing east. He had heard the call to prayer.

"They just don't listen," he said.

"No, they don't," I concurred, "and they never will. We're doomed."

The blind team cuffed us twelve–zero. I could see their parents jumping with glee, their fabulous faces adorned with trendy spectacles and gleeful smiles.

"Who are these people?" I asked. "A team bred from opticians?"

I looked directly at the slaughtering sun until my eyes went white. If I went blind, maybe I would see things differently. At least I might do enough damage to get a pair of fancy specs, and join the successful team.

"Well done, boys! Well played! Better luck next time! Who are ya?"

"The Dragons!"

Once again we formed a tunnel of hands for our little engine of losers to run through. They chugged along in a carriage of shoulders, a conga line of soccer-playing crap.

CHAPTER 9

Joining the Suburbanites

What was I doing out there on Saturday mornings, standing on the sideline of a bumpy and poorly maintained soccer field, withered by sleep deprivation, taking part in an exercise that delivered the opposite of success, my supposed suburban goal? If I could not successfully help manage a soccer team and get kids to listen, how would I manage a city hall budget and get the public to hear my voice? My son had seen the writing on the wall, too—all he wanted was to go back to swimming lessons.

My destiny as a coach was linked to the coaching strategy of an Iranian team boss. He picked the team. He made the substitutions. My hands were tied.

There were two ways to go at this point. 1) I could undermine Mahmoud with a parental whispering campaign or 2) I could endeavor to be supportive by being chatty, forcing Mahmoud to speak to me with more than a sentence or a few words. The latter seemed the better of the distasteful options. If we united, and communicated, the team would improve.

If it didn't work out, I still had the option of destroying his reputation before the praetorian parents. But before that eventuality, they would need to feel that I was one of them and not some Scottish freak that was ODD and heading for the shocking headlines from the sidelines. Having my kid in the team was not enough to cement their trust. I needed to be like them. To look and act like them.

I coached in urban thrift shop castoffs and Doc Martens boots, the garb I wore to work. My colors were grim and dark, like black boils. In addition, I often looked like a ghoul. I had no time to shower before games, stumbling from bed minutes before the kickoff. My teeth were brown. My eyes looked like a munitions dump that had just exploded. No wonder people took a giant step back when I approached them. For all I knew, Mahmoud may well have been conversational champion of the year but when he came up against my breath he sought refuge in a quiet cave until the dragon had flown over. I needed to get brushing and set sail for Dockers Island.

"Where do you shop for those clothes?" I asked Mahmoud.

"At the mall," he said.

"I think I might get some of those Dockers. Everyone seems to be wearing them."

I piled into the tin heap and headed to the mall. At JCPenney I headed for the first person I saw folding clothes. Her dark plump hair fitted her bright plump body.

"I'm looking for the Dockers section. I need the whole

wardrobe. Slacks, shirts, shorts, socks, belts. Do you know if they do underarm antiperspirant? Cologne? Do they do Y-fronts?"

She stepped back a yard.

What was she thinking? Security?

She tentatively walked to the nifty Dockers sign hanging on the wall.

"Here you are. All the Dockers lines are here. These ones are Go Khaki with Stain Defender," she said, pointing at a pile.

"I bet you President Clinton wished Monica had been wearing these," I said.

"Changing rooms to the back," she replied, seemingly confused.

"Thank you," I growled.

I riffled quickly through the selection as if I meant business but I tried to remain outwardly casual. First off the rack were the white cotton Dockers pants. I grabbed a blue golf shirt and tossed a pair of the khaki shorts on top. I changed into the pants in a changing room and looked in the mirror. My groin drain opened, my libido went down the plughole, and my sex was washed out to sea. These pants were designed as a conspiracy to preserve low birth rates and save social security. The crotch must have been sprayed with the mythical saltpeter tablets that they gave to inmates and soldiers. An erection was impossible in this tactile tundra. No wonder middle-aged suburban males in Dockers were besieging doctors for solutions to their under-par boners.

I tried on the golf shirt. Instantly, tits appeared.

"These are fucking horrible," I said.

I went to find the assistant.

"Are these made in China?" I asked her.

"I don't know, why does it matter?"

"Because these are a conspiracy to keep the American shag pile cut low."

She took two steps backward.

I marched back into the cubicle and pulled on the khaki shorts. Instant butt itch! A pair of these would give you hemorrhoids in a week, so besides Viagra you would be stocking the medicine cabinet with Preparation H or, if you disliked the feeling of cream between your buns, employing the wire brush and alcohol. I panicked. The store music suddenly sounded like Chopin's Death March, that song they played at Soviet leader funerals. This was the end of who I was. These Dockers were very, very dangerous pants indeed.

Back out in the store proper I yelled over to the employee, who was now at a distance greater than normal conversation allowed. "I'll take the slacks and the shirt but I'll forgo the shorts. And I need some loafers."

"I'm doing this to help my community," I told the cashier.

I tried on my new outfit in front of the mirror at home. I was strangled by it. In terror, I squeezed my shrunken balls. Damn! Worse than steroids! The sacrifice I was making! I had the clothes of suburban man, and the shoes. It was the first step toward coming out of the suburbanite closet. But there were more deficiencies needing fixed if I was to fit in and be fully accepted as a member of the tribe.

First, I needed the bland haircut, the boring businesslike snip that signaled my commitment to uniformity. I was faced with a difficult decision: Should I embrace the neutron bomb of hairstyles, the Bill Gates job, or keep my hip, proto-Mod style. This choice frightened me. And besides, I suffered from a chronic condition—something akin to emotional dandruff—when it came to haircuts. I had diagnosed myself as suffering from PHSD—post-haircut stress disorder— which had been inflicted upon me in childhood by the local barber from my hometown.

His name was Desi Divers, the Barber of Glasgow, a tragic operator. Back in the seventies, Desi Divers Barber Shop was up a small stairway in an old brick building on our Main Street. He shared the premises with a hair salon for women. Salons were segregated back then. To get to his section, men were forced to pass by rows of ladies' heads humming inside conical hair dryers. I always thought it looked like aliens had landed. Once you reached the men's section, you were in a different world. You knew that your barber would keep your secrets to himself: dandruff, psoriasis, and scabs, and then maybe money troubles, girls you fancied, whether or not you were Catholic or Protestant. He was like your doctor. Sadly, in Desi Diver's case, he was Dr. Mengele.

Desi's corner had two large barber chairs facing the mirrors. Broken music crackled from an old radio, too low to make out. Big black combs floated in superblue disinfectant gel jars, like fetuses. A two-bar electric fire on the wall baked the room like a pizza oven. Desi did his thing amid the cigarette smoke and hacking coughs. Clippers buzzed between the sounds of the snip-snip. No one spoke. In fact, the only word I ever heard Desi say was "Next."

"I want it short at the back, but over the ears, and a side parting," I would say.

Desi was dressed in blue overalls pocked with the grease stains of a million dandruff-ridden hairs. He always wore a clean dress shirt and a tightly wound necktie. His own hairstyle was experimental, a great wash of hair curving round the back of his head like a wave.

But the most appalling aspect of this barbaric fiend was his attack on children's hair. His face had the calmness of a mannequin, and the message in his eyes was as clear as day: *I feel nothing.* So no matter what instructions you gave Desi, all children walked out of his hairy laboratory sporting the German Helmet cut, circa 1933–45.

As I sat being clipped and buzzed back into the Second World War, a low whistle came from Desi's mouth, out of tune and dripping with pure menace. He was whistling "The Great Escape."

Once freed from the chair of torture, I quickly paid and pondered my best route home. A tunnel under the city, direct to my house, would have been ideal. But there was to be no escaping people's gazes and what I imagined they thought: *Desi's made another German.* So I slid along the walls of buildings, trying to get home unnoticed. I turned my face away from shop windows. On the way, I looked up at the town hall, to where the Union Jack, the flag of the Queen, was flying from the staff. Why was Desi so unpatriotic? Why didn't he cut us all into the shape of a British soldier's helmet?

"Please take me to the other barber on the Main Street," I begged my mum when I finally got home. "All the other kids are going there now."

She was having none of it. "Desi's cheap and the ends don't split," she said.

"But I look like a Nazi!" I cried.

"Don't be stupid," she said. "You don't look anything like a Nazi. I remember the war, don't forget. You look like Alan."

I still had school to negotiate, and it never went well after a trip to Desi's. Walking through the halls I was dimly aware of whispered jolts of *Sieg Heil* from my schoolmates. Even "wee men" tried it on.

My anger needed an outlet, and I found it on the soccer field. I hacked the other team with mercilessly high challenges, two-footed assaults that left some in tears, others in wheelchairs. I didn't just "leave my foot in" tackles, I actually inserted my entire body, including muddy cleats, up the derrieres of unsuspecting goalkeepers. I screamed orders, clicked my heels, and stomped on the squishy bits of my generation. Eventually I'd grow tired and retreat back to the classroom, where I'd subvert the cardinal rule and make threats only to kids I knew I could beat in a fight.

Out in the street after school I would berate dogs, chase

cats, and laugh at people's disabilities. It would be years before I learned the word for it, but this was schadenfreude at its most clinical.

It would take several weeks for the German Helmet to grow out. In that time, I laughed at crippled people, ended the lives of bugs and flies, and was generally out of sorts. It was good training, I suppose, for a season coaching the Dragons.

Nevertheless, I put my childhood fears behind me and got up the courage to get my haircut. I found a—wait for it—*female* barber in my neighborhood.

I walked into her salon and saw glass jars with combs in them. Holy shit! The lights were blinding. Heads that looked severed sat on top of black coveralls, trimmed, shaved, swept. The conical hair dryer had landed in the corner. Music played from a radio.

"I will make your hair nice for you," she said, as my body disappeared under the black coverall.

"Just don't cut it like a helmet," I told her. "I want the easy listening haircut. You know what I mean. I want to look like Bill Gates."

"Is his hair real?" she asked.

I closed my eyes and drifted into thought. I could hear the snip and buzz, and feel her soft hands sifting through my mane. The trance of the haircut took over, the grooming, the joy of being a monkey.

I popped open my eyes. Relief! I looked like a square.

It was the perfect haircut for a job in boring software development. But I still needed one more necessity to complete my suburbanite profile. I needed that American smile.

No one had ever got elected without one. Jimmy Carter. Ronald Reagan. Bill Clinton. Popularity depended on it. It was the signature on the success checks. Mahmoud had one, and he used it expertly. It was his parent disposal, his calming tool, disarming angry explosions ignited by his lousy coaching and results. Where had he got that smile? At the mall?

Much like my cussing problem, I was at a major disadvantage in this department. Being Scottish, I had grown up in a cloudy country under the reign of English television. You had to laugh or else you'd cry. But people rarely smiled. Notwithstanding the candy, soda, and cookie culture worshipped in Scotland, many rows of teeth were spoiled by genetic crooks or had been burgled altogether. My Scottish scowl was environmentally produced. Rain clouds were heavy things. They sat on your head, forcing the facial features down. And I was doing myself no favors in the smile department by earning my living in a neighborhood where the American smile was, if not already dead, at best on life support.

I sought professional guidance on this tricky smiling matter.

I asked the team psychiatrist.

"Dr. John, everyone seems to be able to smile on demand. I'm Scottish. Is there any hope?"

"It takes exercise. Smiling is an unconscious/conscious discipline; it takes work to perfect it and when the moment arrives you know it instinctively. This triggers the cheeks into motion."

"Like this," I said.

He retreated.

"Eh . . . yes . . . kinda," he replied.

The aim was to smile when there was absolutely nothing to smile about. That was the American way. But it defied the law of emotional physics to see the parents' cheeks rise in glee, as they patted their Dragons on the head and beamed *Well done* after a defeat of incalculable measure. Were they working their cheeks in a gymnasium? Was there a cheek-lifting machine? Maybe I would buy some feet clamps and suspend myself from the ceiling, allowing my cheeks to fall to the center of the earth with gravity's unbending help.

But I was not a bat.

How about the talking cure? I could see the doctor and cry and sob and say, "Help me, Doctor, I'm so unhappy, I'm unable to sleep, I haven't smiled in years, I'm addicted to miserable late-night televangelist shows and I have to suffer under the tutelage of an Iranian soccer boss with a big grin and he makes veiled threats in a foreign language that sound like he might be in Al Qaeda or something, and I hear voices saying I'm worthless and I can't laugh either and people say to me day in and day out why don't you smile and I just can't take it anymore."

And then there was the final desperate solution: Scotch tape. This is how it worked. Stick five layers of the tape on the top of the cheeks and wrap it over the top of your head, attaching it to the back of the neck. Secure the bond by wrapping more Scotch tape around your neck but be careful not to make the noose too tight, as the goal is to make a smile and not a death mask. Sure enough, the edges of the mouth will rise. The forces of lift will defy the forces of melancholia. Soon you will be able to throw the antidepressants in the trash and lead a successful smiling American life.

CHAPTER : 10

Body Parts

It was three past the witching hour. The only other light on was the moon. Raccoons and skunks prowled outside and the miserable turgid waves of Arkansas preaching were blaring on the set. The Murrays never smiled. I presumed it was against their religion. The day those two broke out the ivory would be the day Jesus returned in a dentist's jacket.

"It's time to solve my smile problem," I told Ben and Jerry, sitting on my lap, smiling at me as I ate the dead part of the Grateful Dead. They raised their cones. The cat was purring, grinning ear to ear as it slurped on the cremated ashes of another finished Cherry Garcia.

"Even Steven the cat is smiling," I said, as I reached for the aptly named Scotch tape. It was no use. The Newtonian forces of *miserabilia* sank my cheeks and caused the tape at the back of my head to catch on my neck hair, prompting me to shout, "Ahhh . . . fer fuck sake!" which nearly woke up the sleeping household and scared the cat so much that it spewed up a hairball on the rug, once it had landed.

At the next game I wore the Dockers and the loafers but left the Scotch tape at home. I creaked onto the soccer field, horribly self-conscious, convinced that my sperm count was wiped and that my hair would fall out within months. I decided to approach a mom supporting the other team and practice a brave new smile in my brave new world of fashion. I chose her because her smile could have been used to make shipping safe.

That said, there was something a little too tight about her body parts. Her gorgeous red lips looked like large trampolines. Her face was preserved by a skin-styled cling film, her youth kept fresh with ever-increasing tension stretches. This woman would never be an old potato with popped eyes and divots desecrating her appeal. Also, there was no boob jiggle. Her beacons shone through her blouse.

"You're so smiley," I said. "That's great."

I broke out the brown-toothed smile.

She beamed.

And leaned backward.

"I'm the coach with the other team. We've had a terrible season. We've lost every game. The parents are bad, the other coach is terrible, and the kids don't seem to be enjoying it."

She smiled.

"And it's a nightmare getting here, trapped in the traffic. My knees are killing me."

She smiled.

"And then you get here and the kids never listen."

This woman would smile through hail, snow, hurricanes,

tsunamis, nuclear attacks, and adventure novels. I imagined her being chased by a halitosis beast covered in gingivitis scales, ultimately to be saved by a hero with a sword and crest on his shield.

The shine of her smile was getting painful, so I crossed over to the other side of the field, where Mahmoud was chatting to the parents. I beamed hello. Silence; I pushed on—they had to accept me. But there was nothing in my conversational portfolio that appealed to these people. I had heard them talk expertly about stock options, start-ups, software, markets, travel, and private school tuition. As a veteran bartender, what were my conversational gambits? Well, I knew exactly what kind of alcohol a person had drunk by looking at their vomit. I could tell if a man entering a room was drunk by the way he opened a door. I could sniff out a fight five minutes before it started. But none of this would do in suburban California.

Instead, I made a point of shaking my legs, hoping that they would notice the Dockers. The Dolt in Need of a Volt's dad looked at me blankly. I chatted him up, praising his son's marvelous goalkeeping skills in the last double-digit defeat.

"He's a good learner," said the Dolt's dad.

"What does he want to be when he grows up?" I said. "An electrician?"

"No. An architect."

That made sense. He was like a building when he played soccer. He just fucking stood there.

"Let's hope we can get a win today and the bad luck lightning doesn't strike us again," I said.

"Hey, you're Scottish, right?"

Why deny it?

"Yeah, that's right."

"You must love golf—all you Scots do; you invented the game. You must have played St. Andrews?"

"Many times," I said, my smile a bad lie in the rough.

I hated golf. It was Freudian horror, all those little balls with holes.

THE SPORTING GREEN

FUNEREAL DISEASE

This journalist is having a hard time finding anything new to say about the Dragons. How can I continue reporting on this totem pole of grotesque defeat? My experience covering this season has reduced my sports-writing skills to the point that I've applied for the job as the chief obituary writer at this newspaper. The Dragons have driven me there.

The Dragons funeral is now, and it's a horrible sight: The unbearable image of a child's coffin being carried to the grave on the shoulders of the shite and the Shi'ite. A single pink flower is being lowered on the casket to the depths of soccer oblivion. From Hades, a hostile gust rides across the cemetery and blows the shite and the Shi'ite into the grave alongside their tragic team.

Game 5 was the ultimate game of death. The Dragons' new goalkeeper, the Dolt in Need of a Volt, to give him his full name, conceded a tidal wave of goals, the ball washing through his legs and arms, jolting over his head and around his body. The only noble gesture left, for Coach Mahmoud and Assistant Coach Black, is to salute and go down with the ship.

Coach Black put a torpedo in the tube and again attacked his players during his postgame conference with the media:

"These players are the worst I have ever seen. It's like coaching statues and zombies. This generation of kids seems to have changed the frequency on us. They don't listen to good common sense from men who know. It's not good enough for the players to say that they don't understand what is being said to them. Iran and Scotland are not countries on the dark side of the moon. We are speaking English to them. Coach Mahmoud is beginning to wonder if this is some kind of religious punishment, a loser's plague. Have we annoyed Zeus so much that he has sent Apollo to strike us down with poisoned arrows?"

CHAPTER 11

New Seeds

I pulled out the Gideon's Bible I had liberated from a motel room and began looking through the testaments for sporting advice. There was no mention of soccer, surprising when you considered the number of Italians walking around Judea at the time of Jesus. And with heads being served on plates, a kick around would have been the natural extension of decapitation.

From the barn in Arkansas, Reverend Murray mentioned the word "seed," a dangerous germ of a word, likely to cause holy havoc. There was Adam's seed, the devil's seed, Cain and Abel, the evil and the good. Planting or spilling seed, it was all the same. Roots sunk, shoots fired up, bellies swelled, and soon the world was a tangled, knotted mess of unwanted weeds and abandoned children.

Dear Reverend Murray,

I have read the Old and New Testaments through and cannot find any reference to a sprawling tribe called the

Suburbanites. But they do exist and they are out here in California and they have planted their seeds and are taking over many acres of our land. These Suburbanites might be other places too, but I don't get out to the heartland of the country much and cannot say for sure if any of these Suburbanites have spread or been cast out of the golden land, but if you see them when you go outside your barn (although you might not go out much like me) you might want to look out for garments marked with the label of these beasts, an anchor with a rope around it. These modern Suburbanites are the enemy of the one true Christ. They are dragging America down to the bottom of the ocean. And my team of Dragons is still losing all our games and I now know that this is a test by God. He tested Job and that is who I am, I am Job doing a job that's hard. Please, please pray for the Dragons and the corruption of the seed from the Suburbanites.

Yours faithfully,
Alan Black—a fellow Scot

Later, the sun baked the earth. I stood staring at my homestead lawn, the stamp of suburban man. My lawn was seriously ill. It had a fever, scabby lesions were breaking out across its surface, and weed tumors were munching away at the heart of the green. I touched it. It was sticky, and icky, like the carpet in a by-the-hour motel. How the fuck had this happened? It was fine and dandy until I started coaching the Dragons.

Across the street, my neighbor with a Jarhead haircut sneered at me. His triumvirate of gas guzzler, small boat, and virile lawn complemented the large American flag flying from his porch. Every day he watered. Hired hands gave his lawn a regular military trim. His laryngitic dog pooped on my ruined patch, passing judgment. The trash collector told me, "You've killed that lawn." A friend sympathized. "Your poor sod, you poor sod," he said, as he let a handful of lawn ashes fall through his fingers. It was lawn murder in the first degree. In my mind's eye I saw the Lawn Ranger come galloping down my street, where he proceeded to hang me from a lamppost.

I thought of the Dragons. Their rot had spread to my grass. But I was determined not to surrender. I pledged there and then that my lawn, and my team, would recover. It would be the greatest comeback since Lazarus. From Home Depot I'd get seeds, fertilizer, and weed killer. I'd subscribe to *Lawn and Leisure* magazine and turn this dying scab of earth into a fertile oasis, a symbol of American success.

And the Dragons would have a glorious comeback, too. I would apply the same solutions to them. More aggressive berating of the players; root out the weeds, like the prehistoric fern, and replace the rest of the dead stalks with some new talent, if we could find any willing replacements out there in sweet suburbia. The union of new seeds and coaching success—the Murrays would be pleased to hear of such a commitment to spiritual union.

• • • •

At the next practice I said, "Mahmoud, I think we need a new philosophy. We have to be the comeback kids. Remember Clinton said that when he ran for president before the stain defenders got him."

"No," said Mahmoud.

"Well, I'm talking about making some changes to the team, getting new players, ones that can actually play, who want to play, and making the team believe that they are the comeback kids."

"I pick the team," said the Supreme Leader.

"I know but . . ."

"I pick the team. Just keep coaching with what we have."

"That's like asking corpses to get up and dance, Mahmoud."

"I pick the team."

He couldn't pick his fucking nose.

There was little chance of us melding now. What was this power trip he was on? Iran might have got a tie with us back in 1978 but Scotland would bury Iran in a game of soccer today.

I had held back from putting dreadful curses on people all season long. But now the power of the curse that blew up Mr. Roberts's house flew in from the past.

I said to myself, "Mahmoud, I hope you vanish, you horrible Khaki Stain Defender."

· · · · ·

I could not count the number of times my boyhood soccer team had fought hard in the face of defeat. We knew how to kick, tear strips, and crack shins. I gave the "fight them on the beaches" speech so many times, Churchill felt robbed. And sometimes our enemies kicked our heads in, but they never kicked the hope out of us. It was worth every bruise. We called it "getting stuck in."

Mahmoud would never understand that. Fuck Mahmoud. He didn't know what a fight was. He was a spectator, that's what he was best at, that's what he should have been all along. He was no coach. And he could keep his mall smile and cotton Dockers for himself. These fucking sexual insecticide pants would be going in the landfill at the end of the season. I would be getting my Doc Martens back on my feet and wearing my pants blooming with the stains of beer, muck, grime, and working slog.

I thought of starting the whispering campaign now but the parents still recoiled when I approached. Blasted dentistry! All I could do for the team was tell my defenders to ignore Mahmoud. I would belt the idea of fighting back into them until they stopped the onslaught of goals.

I gathered the defenders at practice.

"Now listen. This is the most important thing you will hear this year. See them up there training with Mahmoud? They are not going to score any goals. None. They can't help us. So we need to stop the other team scoring goals against us. And to do that, we are going to kick them off the park. We're going to scare them. Halloween has come early. We're going to get stuck into them!"

"I love Halloween," said the potted plant.

"Put on your masks, kids. Let's scare the sh—sugar out of them on Saturday. It's time to take no prisoners."

Later, I took my son aside and told him, "Don't listen to anything that Mahmoud says. He'll only lead you astray. Get stuck into the enemy and fight for every ball, and fight back against them. Leave a permanent mark on their defenders."

"Can I go to swimming lessons instead?" he said.

• • • •

On the next game day, there was a nip in the air. My skin was bristling, hairs were up straight. I was pacing, dropping to my knees, charged up with the prospect of watching a few shins being cracked, on my orders. Aggression was the motif, the lance that was needed if this season was to be saved. I was sick and tired of retreat. On to Jerusalem! With or without Mahmoud! Immediately after the kickoff I started yelling, "Get stuck in!"

I would yell it a million times.

"Roar for every ball!" I screamed.

"Show him the ground up close!" I bellowed.

The Aztec god was first to apply the method, hacking down the opponents. My kid got the message. He was crunching their defenders' legs and getting cautioned by the referee. Even the prehistoric fern let his petal drop on the head of an attacker. The fat kid, who may or may not have been branded with the name Ashley, had gone unnoticed all season but today he let his belly do the rumbling over the enemy. Drake, the son of the Rasta, now free from the dread and lock of goalie, cracked a few shins.

"That's it," I yelled. "Get stuck into them!"

Mahmoud was silent. The parents looked unsure. But

they saw the defenders fight for once. The score was under double figures for the first time this season. And more importantly, we had gone the entire second half without conceding a goal.

"Well done, you guys," I yelled. "You guys were great. You got stuck in!"

I went around the defenders, roughing their heads.

"I like that 'stuck in' stuff. What's that mean?" said Manny.

We formed the tunnel of hands and our little team of losers, who got stuck in, trundled through to choo-choo whistles. They were going somewhere at last.

"You see, Mahmoud. You have to fight back. You have to believe that you can come back from the dead. Plant that seed in the attackers."

Now, if I could only get the emotionally redundant vegetables out of the narrative and reseed the plot then I might be able to get a better story out of this season, yet it had to be said, it was the hardest fucking thing I had ever volunteered for. And the seeds of victory were still concealed. Where were they to be found?

THE SPORTING GREEN

FIGHTING DRAGONS IMPROVE

On a wet field, the Dragons sank to their sixth straight loss Saturday in a match against Walnut Creek Select but there was something more to report than a sackload of conceded goals. The Creek opened the scoring after two minutes with a fine shot from outside the penalty box by their top scorer, Brad Wayne. But he was then upended in a crunching tackle by Manny, who seemed to be slobbering at the mouth with a lust for life. Shortly after, Dragons striker Black was cautioned for a wild two-footed sliding tackle that chopped the lumber from Walnut Creek defender Bush. Three minutes later, Zalohexagonal [*sic*], for the Dragons, body-checked Creek's Hunter, causing him to vomit.

Walnut Creek inevitably took control of the game but not without the Dragons leaving a few more stains on their defenders. In the nineteenth minute, Wayne scored his second goal and completed his hat trick a minute later with a fine strike from all of six yards. In the twentieth minute, Walnut Creek midfielder Brat Bradley opened his account with a wonderful diving header. His second came two minutes later and his hat trick was complete thirty seconds after the Dragons kicked off.

The Dragons made some changes for the second half, bringing on the defender Ashley. He had been out of the squad since the forgotten early chapters of the season and his impact seemed to stem the flow. For the first time this year, the Dragons went a half without conceding a goal. It was quite remarkable to see an attacking team thwarted by a rough defense, seemingly energized by the idea of taking legs instead of the ball.

At the postmatch press conference, Coach Lloyd Regan of the Creek said, "It's a result but I'm not happy with the second-half performance. We need more commitment from our players, and as I said before the game, it's always difficult to come here and play because the state of the field is the biggest danger you face. The pitch could easily have beaten us today. We're not used to that kind of rutted field out where we live in the whites-preferred suburbs. And the violent nature of some of the Dragons' play was reprehensible at times, quite shocking in its viciousness."

Assistant Coach Black, standing in for Coach Mahmoud, who stormed off at the end of the game, issued a warning to future visiting teams.

"All season long teams have come down here guaranteed a win but today in the second half, we showed that we can stand up to pressure. Our boys showed that we are no pushovers, so take note. If you come to play the Dragons and think that we are going to lie down like lambs to the slaughter, then think again. You had better bring your medical kit, your splints, your health insurance, and your ambulance because when we finish with you that will be your mode of transport home. Who are we? We're the Fighting Dragons, the hardest crew in the division."

At the end of the press conference reporters handed a copy of his statement to the police.

CHAPTER 12

Good Coach

Lawn and leisure were the perfect suburban combo. This was surely what the founding fathers dreamed of when they imagined a future filled with Fourth of July barbecues on the lawn, the pursuit of happiness. Leisure was the highest state of development for American spirituality. Men even wore the word in suit form back in the seventies. And there was a magazine that unified the two. I found a copy of *Lawn and Leisure* magazine at my local newsstand. In it, I read a helpful piece by the Weed Man and a feature story headline that was a metaphor for my coaching journey with the Dragons: Voyages with Vegetables.

I stood on my lawn with my bag of seeds. My weed killer had delivered its chemical weaponry several days before. I had soared over the archipelagos of black weeds and bombed them from the air.

"Take this, you bastards. Here's some chemotherapy for ya!" I said.

And now it looked as if the cancer was in remission; the

black patches had gone bald. This lawn would soon have a head of hair again as the green locks were destined to return. I went for the hose. A dribble of water came forth. I tried to untangle the knot in the line but it suddenly ruptured and a shot of spray soaked me. The remaining stalks of green grass on the lawn leaned desperately forward with outstretched blades, hoping that a droplet would fill their gasping parched throats. It was sad, very sad.

The neighbor across the street was watering his plants with a flush from his power hose, showing off the tempo and the water design by rotating his fancy hose head. His wee, busty wife stood on the steps watching him with his hose in hand. She smiled, completely satisfied.

His Stars and Stripes were fluttering in the breeze. *Damn him,* I thought. I went inside my house and retrieved my Scotland flag, the one I wore around my shoulders when Scotland played England at soccer. I made a little flagpole out of a stick and planted St. Andrew's Cross in the middle of my crucified lawn.

"Take that, Yankee," I said under my breath.

"Hi," I yelled across the street.

His hose hissed and he wrapped up his snake and followed his wife into the house.

I jumped in the car, headed to Home Depot, and returned with a hose.

I stopped at Noah's Bagels for my breakfast. Noah made the bagels on-site, dishing out the flavors, the lox, and the cream cheese to all of us who had descended from those lucky enough to have gotten a berth on the ark. The bustle of early morning was over by the time I arrived for my daily bread, and I stood looking at warm cream cheese slither forth from my poppy seed bagel. It dropped on the floor, pooling. I thought of the Dragons, drowning.

"What do you call this?" I said, holding up my sloppy circle, to a woman next to me.

"Let me guess," she said. "A bagel."

"No. It's a life ring."

"Well, don't let me get in the way of the rescue," she said, trying to be funny.

Being saved was not just a matter for goalkeepers or life guards. Reverend Murray, that brick of Arkansas faith, loved to talk about it. His sermons on the biblical flood and Noah's ark lifted me up.

Dear Reverend Murray,

I appreciate breakfast. I've always seen it as a meta-phor for the resurrection. I avoid late suppers, so often the cause of gastric crucifixion. Joyfully, I had an epiph-any at one such breakfast recently. While standing in Noah's Bagel Shop eating my creamy poppy seed, I dis-covered how Noah had saved the beasts of the earth, those unfortunates that missed the boat. He made a batch of bagels and used them as life rings, throwing them to gi-raffes, lions, and dinosaurs as he sailed along. I thought I would share this wonderful news with you, and the flock, a major contribution to filling in the holes in the middle of Genesis. Please tell your son Dennis that a KFC that

*does a nice bucket has opened near my house, if he ever
wants to come out for a visit to California.*

*Saving souls and Dragons,
Alan Black*

"We're turning the lawn and the season around. It's prophecy," I said to Ben and Jerry and the cat as I sat in my sofa hole. Ben and Jerry shrugged their hippie shoulders as I got stuck into their ice Eric Clapton, Ginger Baker, Jack Bruce. It was four a.m.; the cryptic mind of the drowsy rose from a crossword.

"Fuck! Why don't they read out my letters at the end of the show? Some idiot wants to know if singing is okay in church or does it lead to screwing the minister's wife in the haystack near the barn? What kind of daft theological question is that?"

Steve, the cat, meowed in agreement. I grabbed the remote and fired any combination of numbers to escape the droning bagpipes coming from Arkansas.

And there he was, all things bright and beautiful: the slayer of darkness, Tony Robbins.

• • • •

Here was a man who could deliver results. He was a prime-time example of a good coach. The Personal Power guru was the man for the motivational mission, the man loaded with the ammunition you needed to shoot for success in America. And he was willing to bomb the underachievers and slouch potatoes out of their ruts if they were willing to drop a few hundred bucks into his fat bank account for his DVD series. I tuned in the ear and opened a fresh bag of insomnia and a can of Dutch lager. Maybe he could help me with some new techniques to coach more aggression into the team.

From a sunny beach somewhere in paradise, a curvy TV celebrity who had come under his spell was introducing him. Robbins bounded onto the stage, alert and jazzed.

His words flew off his big chin like F-16s leaving the deck of an aircraft carrier. Robbins was going to sink our doubts and rescue us with his flotilla of coaching perfection.

"Throw me the rope, Tony," I yelled.

Robbins's smile was as bright as the Lighthouse at Alexandria. But he was a wonder of the modern world. He whipped his arms around in huge flowing movements. He was a one-man turbine, a superb human example of renewable energy. He was the answer to the energy crisis. This guy could keep the lights on in New York for a week just by waving his arms.

I turned Ben and Jerry around so that they could see the screen.

"See that. That's what you call an American success story. He's helped people get motivated. He's coached losers to victory. You two fat bastards have only made diabetes more popular."

The hands on the clock on the wall were ready to give a high five but not before Tony Robbins had high-fived every disciple in the front row of the outdoor location somewhere in paradise. To motivate others was the greatest fuel of all, for then you were the source of life itself. This was the goal of the coach. I got off the sofa. It was time to follow the leader.

"Here goes," I said to the cat.

I rubbed my nose until it shone. Meanwhile, Robbins was gallivanting around the stage with his arms stretched up like a boxer after winning a bout. The sails of the crowd were filling with motivation. They were poised to receive the blow that would propel them to success. I opened my arms and swept them up and round, like a mad helicopter trying to take off at five a.m., with a destination for success. I traversed the living room floor, swishing and swooshing, whacking the air, my pajamas stuck to my legs like ballet tights.

"You can do it, Dragons!" I yelled, "Get stuck in! You can score a goal!"

I launched myself into the air and attempted a *grand jeté*. I landed with a thud, stubbing my toe off the blasted cat, which let out a mangled ball-of-fur shriek.

"Aaaah, fer fuck sake! Get out of my fucking road."

Robbins was yelling into his mike as I collapsed back into the sofa puffing and holding my hurt extremity.

"You can! You can! You can!" he said.

I picked up the Dutch lager, downed it, and went to bed rejuvenated, ready to put my finger in the dyke and save the season with my Personal Power. I was determined to save the Dragons and be a good coach.

HALFTIME

CHAPTER 13

Going South

"**H**ave you heard of Tony Robbins?" I asked.

"Is he in the team?" said the Kurd, Speedy's father.

"No. He coaches people, a life coach. He waves his arms around and creates a wind like a big turbine and the audience seems to get motivated by it. I think I'm going to try that with the team on Saturday at the next game."

"It sounds like a good idea," he said. "More wind."

I bent over and scanned his face for signs of Kurdish sarcasm.

He went on, "By the way, there's no game on Saturday. The game has been rescheduled. There's a break in the season."

"How do you know?"

"Mahmoud called and told me."

"Where's Mahmoud?"

"He's not here."

"I guess you can be assistant for today's practice then," I offered.

"There's no practice. It's canceled. I'm just here walking my dog. I live around here."

"Why didn't someone tell me?" I said.

"I don't know. I don't run the team."

•   •   •   •

We were about halfway through the season, and with the unexpected break, I had a chance to reflect on everything that had gone wrong. And halftime offered an opportunity to rekindle the coaching fire, the fire that I was going to set under Mahmoud's ass for not telling me the practice was off, and the season was on hold.

Halftime had other precious moments, too. It was a chance to relieve oneself. Since the season began, I felt like I had been holding it all in. Now I could let the pressure off, release the strain. As a kid, I had watched men at soccer games urinate into empty beer cans, unable to control the bladder, but unwilling to go before halftime in case they missed a goal. Sometimes they would throw the smelly can aimlessly in the air, prompting a melee, fights, and an unasked-for golden shower.

•   •   •   •

Nature called me from sunny San Diego. I would take a break and rejuvenate my batteries by visiting America's most beautiful city. A million miles away from dodgy beer cans, this pleasant oasis was my second American home. My in-laws lived there. We were due a visit. My wife and kids flew down early. I stayed at home for a few days scraping the dung off my work body and examining the lawn. I had been unleashing the Gorgon's head of water on the soil for days. I could not see the seeds. I hoped they had gone underground to fertilize. I pulled on a pair of golf shoes that I had picked up at a garage sale and stomped all over the . . . I couldn't say green. The guy at Home Depot had suggested it.

"Golf shoes are good for aerating," he said.

I made tiny holes. I felt weird.

With the beach ball in one hand, and my bucket and spade in the other, I turned on the burglar alarm and headed to the airport.

* * * * *

Straight to the beach on landing, I floated upside down on the ocean, and then flipped over and floated facedown, hoping the lifeguard would see me and make a rescue, *Baywatch*-style. I always fancied being taken back to dry land on top of Pamela Anderson's flotation devices. But there was no joy today. I came up for air. The lifeguard had gone to lunch.

On my last trip to SoCal, I had witnessed a rescue. The lifeguard had jumped over rocks and plunged into the angry surf, which was busy swallowing a struggling fool for dinner. Mesmerized landlubbers watched as the seal-like lifeguard sped through the froth, tied a line to the drowning man, and returned him to safety. What struck me was the lack of interest the lifeguard showed in the applause he received. He went back to his duty, sitting in his tower, a perfect example of leadership.

Now that the Dragons were sinking beneath the tidal wave of humiliation, could a rescue even be attempted? Would the parents applaud if it was pulled off? I was not like the heroic lifeguard. I would take a bow and say, "Remember this act of soccer salvation when it comes to voting for me in the mayoral election. If I can turn shite into gold on a soccer field, think what I can do with a city hall budget."

• • • •

I couldn't find the Arkansas Murray boys at the Shepherd's Chapel on the San Diego cable but the place was teeming with bumper stickers proclaiming that everybody's boss was a Jewish carpenter. I saw one rebel vehicle that asked, CAN I HAVE YOUR CAR AFTER THE RAPTURE? It was hot. It was dusty. And the lawns were perfect green.

I had a chat with my mother-in-law's neighbor.

"Hi," I said with a smile, improving due to a miracle product, the teeth-whitening strip.

He looked scared, as if he had never met another human being.

"Yes?"

"I'm visiting from Northern California and I'm having a spot of bother with my lawn. How do you keep it so green?"

"Are you a foreigner?"

"No, I'm an American."

"You don't sound American."

"I am Scottish and I am an American."

"Scottish?"

"Yes, like Mel Gibson; you know—*Braveheart, The Passion of the Christ.*"

"Yes."

"How do you keep the lawn green?"

"Sprinkler system. On a timer. I got it off Rain Bird."

"Rain Bird?"

"World leader. Irrigation systems."

"And it works. What about seed?"

"Seed?"

"Yes, seed."

"Oh, no. I don't know anything about that. You said Northern California. Are you from San Francisco?"

"Around there."

"A lot of weirdos up there."

I put my arm on my hip.

"Yes, sir. Weirdos everywhere."

That did the trick. Gone.

The next day, I pulled onto a San Diego freeway past a dated Christmas billboard that read, JESUS IS THE REASON FOR THE SEASON (and there I was mistakenly thinking it was Macy's). The freeway lanes were wide enough to handle the ever-increasing waistline of the American truck. I drove the rental car to a park, listening to Limbaugh on the radio, wondering what it felt like to drive high on hillbilly heroin.

The biggest-ass vehicles I had ever seen were bursting

over the white belts of the car park spaces. A man in a giant throbbing Hummer was vibrating as he blasted modern country through his music system. If you listened closely enough, you could just make out the sound of a frozen ice shelf shaking and drips falling off it, somewhere up near the North Pole.

Kids and their parents were swarming over the lot like a rash and soon soccer was being played all over. What a contrast to the fields the Dragons were playing on six hundred miles north! These were obviously maintained by squads of excellent gardeners clipping the stalks to perfect heights. There was not a large hole to be found, no rut to twist the ankle in, the perfection unspoiled by no scabby earth weed popping up like beastly acne on a pauper's pitted skin. This turf was as sharp as a Camp Pendleton haircut.

And there they were, the white San Diegan version of suburban parents. The Dockers were on; advanced dermatology was keeping the cancer at bay; blond ponytails popped out above the adjustable strap of baseball caps, some blessed with messages from God. Kids were hopping around with "Jesus Is My Homeboy" T-shirts crucified to their bodies. These people would drive over you in their family wagons if you even thought about doing harm to this paradise.

I took two extra-strength aspirin to kill the throbbing headache Limbaugh had given me. I was glad that I had packed the Stain Defenders and the golf shirt as I stepped out of the car into the glare.

My hairy Scottish ass was sweaty. It was too hot out here.

I looked into the distance and saw a man-made lake stocked with fish. On it, I could see a little boat floating and if I stood in the sun much longer I would see the mirage of a white man with a beard, long hair, and sandals dumping fish into the lake, preparing to host the feeding of the five thousand.

Turning away, I found the soccer moms. They were exceedingly happy and busy with their chat. They munched like happy squirrels, their eyes relaxed. I figured they weren't scared of me, so I introduced myself.

"Hi. How are you today?"

"Good! Hi! I'm Cindy."

"Cindy. That's a great name. I'm Alan. My sister had a doll called Cindy."

"Really? I detect an accent."

"Braveheart."

"Oh, Scottish."

"It's a bit hairy," I said, "especially for the English. I love the scene when the Scots show the English their butts."

"Is your son playing?" she said.

"No. I'm visiting from Northern California. I thought I would check out some local kids' soccer. I'm a coach up there. My team is rubbish. They lose every game."

"Oh, no! You have to have faith."

"I do," I said. "I have faith that we'll lose every game."

"No! You can turn it around. There's always hope."

"The fields look like beautiful green carpets," I said. "The setting is gorgeous. What's the biggest challenge you have down here?"

"Oh, I don't know. Getting the stains out of the uniform and socks."

"You must use a lot of bleach. I see they play in white."

It was the color of the Lord.

I sucked on a lollipop and watched the game for a while. The teams were athletic and well trained, older than the Dragons, teenagers. They had cohesion and discipline. The coaches were well mannered and respectful, and nicely dressed in khaki shorts, white socks, and sneakers. They had clipboards. And they were men; they always were.

The game stopped. A kid was down injured, writhing on the ground in agony, holding his leg. Both coaches ran on to aid the youngster. The player's grimace was a tight one, and he could not stand up. There was no magic sponge to make him better; I thought for a minute that he'd actually broken his leg. He lay around for a bit, then suddenly, as if by magic, he was fine.

Little shite.

I had seen it all before. Pretending you were injured to waste time and deceive the referee was a standard soccer move. As a kid, I had fully mastered the art of faking injury. Muscle cramps were my forte, tightening up the calf and gritting the teeth. Back spasms were my other trick. And when the coach substituted me because my game was not on that day, I would instantly develop a marvelous limp.

Naturally, I would never suggest to any of the Dragons under my command that they should in any way attempt to cheat the referee by faking injury. This was wrong and violated the spirit of positive coaching methods. Not that it mattered. The Dragons would never employ time wasting as a tactic to preserve a lead, as we would never have one, so the only reason to fall over in demented fake agony was to take away vital minutes, limiting the time the opposing team had to score against us. And that was as bleak and depressing as it could get.

I walked over to the injured kid, who been substituted out of the game. He was now sitting on the sidelines.

"What happened?" I asked him.

"My leg got hurt," he said.

I smiled and winked knowingly. Oddly, he looked perplexed, and it struck me that he may actually have been hurt. Just as I was about to say something, the referee blew for the end of the game, and he jumped up, ran onto the field, and joined his teammates on their knees in a prayer circle.

Little shite.

●　●　●　●

I couldn't stand all this sanctity, so when my family went to La Jolla for the day, I went somewhere else: namely, to Tijuana, that great, mad border town, filled with silver-bearing merchants attacking tourists with the plunder of the mines, and beggars with spines that spooked like the crescent moon, holding out meager trembling fingers hoping for a cast-off copper. The sidewalks cracked under the strain of forgotten revolutions; armed *federales* patrolled, waiting to shoot dead for any excuse.

There was a distinct lack of green lawns on the shanty slums on the hillside. Nevertheless, I noticed some boys were playing soccer on a ratty back of earth. I stopped to watch the game at its roots, a street game where the will to fight hard and win rose from the elements. It was spontaneous, energetic, and marvelous. Mexican lads flashed grins and spun firing shots at corrugated poles stuck in the ground as goalposts. The dust hovered and twirled like small tornadoes as the ball sped over the surface, chased like a doomed animal. The ball was used and battered.

In all likelihood these boys would never play on the quilts of green to the north, never have a net to score in, never see a painted line on their pitch, never drive in a car with their parents to play soccer with their mates, never see a referee, never whine, never care less about soccer, all the never that they were destined to carry, and one thing was for certain: they would never be shite at *fútbol*.

I felt a bond with these Mexican lads. I played most of my childhood soccer on a sloping street next to my house. Jackets were the goalposts. We played in our cleats on the tarmac. It helped us slide into tackles with alarming lateness, prompting spectacular aerial somersaults from the victims of the attempted ugly challenges. It was good practice for the real thing. And it made us fit, though our knees grew such heavy scabs it was sometimes hard to run.

I needed a drink. A nearby bar beckoned me with buckets of Corona and tequila. The place was pounding with party animals but I ignored the roars and watched the Mexican soccer on the massive screen.

I had seen four World Cups on television, since moving to the States. All of them in Spanish on the Univision channel. My Spanish language skills were limited to ordering a burrito but no matter. The excitement in the voices of the sportscasters snared me. By contrast, the dreadful English-speaking commentary on ESPN was enough to make you turn the channel to ESPN2 for 6,789 laps of NASCAR. The Mexicans knew how to do soccer on the telly. Nobody did it better.

At halftime, the male studio presenters stood in a made-for-TV barroom surrounded by gorgeous women in hip-hugging soccer strips. The *mujeres hermosas* posed with *pelotas grandes* in their hands. With the mariachi band strumming their pangs in the background, the women toed the balls off camera, as if into your happy lap. A whistle blew, the wiggles began, the shakes and the salsas, the cries of *Viva Mexico!* like revolution breaking out, and soccer and sex thrust outward from the studio to the stadium, where the match commentator sprayed his throat in expectation of the climax . . .

Gooooooaaaaaallllll!!!!!!! Con pasión!

"I'm coaching a soccer team in the States," I told the bartender as I sucked down the bucket of Coronas. "We played a team of Mexicans—they killed us!"

"Americans know nothing about *fútbol*," he said.

"I'm a bartender, too," I replied.

"*Salud! Cin cin!*" he said, pouring me a shot of wild tequila and grabbing my dollars in one smooth action.

"I fucking love Mexico!" I said to the guy next to me. "What *fútbol* team do you support?"

"The San Diego Chargers," he said.

Before making my somewhat wobbly way back to join the great snake with its nose in the air, slowly heading north, I purchased a Mexican soccer strip. I put on the green in the middle of their craziest city, *como un gringo Escocés*. I wore it as I passed over to *el otro lado*. I showed my U.S. passport, smiled, and said, "Howdy," to La Migra.

They didn't smile.

· · · ·

Returning home to NorCal in my Mexico top, soaring above the great blue ocean, listening to the sure fire of the jet's engines, I popped a free Southwest Airlines peanut in my mouth and worried for a brief second about what the parents thought of me as a coach. I was paranoid enough to imagine the indignity of a whispering campaign from people with good teeth and dental insurance. And were they calling each other on the phone? I imagined they must be, by now.

"Hi, Joanie. Can you pick Sam up from soccer practice, I have an appointment at my chiropractor, and I wanted to ask you—what do you think about that Scottish guy coaching the team?"

"Hi, Jen, sure, I'll pick up Sam and drop him off. Yeah, the Scottish guy. He's a joke."

Maybe Mahmoud had got to them first and was blaming me for the team's failure. Would this kill my chances of winning votes from these people? Would suburbanites ever choose a guy who was smile challenged, a cheek-drooping ambitious man of limited vision and questionable temperament? How could I be sure that the players were not saying, "I hate that Scottish guy, Mom. He's a jerk." With such awful thoughts in my mind, for comfort I went back to something much happier. I'm flying at thirty-five thousand feet. And we're all going to die.

THE SECOND
HALF

CHAPTER 14

Back to the Front

The phone was ringing.

"Hello."

"Why are you not at practice? Why are the parents paying the league when the coaches fail to show for training sessions? No one is here to coach the boys!"

The mother of the Aztec god was yelling.

"Practice? I didn't know that there was a practice today."

"Mahmoud is not here. He's gone!"

No one knew Mahmoud's whereabouts. Somewhere in America, an Iranian in a pair of cotton Dockers was unaccounted for.

There was only one thing to do. I got in my car and drove to the training ground.

"Where were you?" asked the maternal guide of the Aztec god.

"Ill," I said, pointing to my head.

"We can't have the boys standing around doing nothing when they should be training. We're paying for it," she said.

She pursed her lips and her neck rose like a snake ready to spit a blast of patchouli oil in my face. The team was sitting on the grass looking abandoned. I strode over to them.

"Get up!" I bawled at them.

"Where were you?" demanded Manny.

"Drunk," I said.

"But that's—"

"Shut up! Get in line."

I went through the motions at the session. The players trotted the balls through the cones, knocking them over as if in training for future DUI arrests. A few sprints round the field followed, then shots at Dolt, which were fluffed, skewered, and limp.

"Dolt! Move it. Get the ball. Put some energy into it."

"Who's Dolt?" asked Manny.

"Just you concentrate on getting stuck in, Manny."

"What's that again?"

"Remember I told you before the break. When they get the ball, you get their guy by tackling him hard and if you don't get the ball make sure that you get him. Line up, team!"

"What?"

"Line up, team!"

"Where?"

"In front of the penalty box."

"Where's that?"

"That box there, the big box."

"That's not a box, it's a field," said Manny.

"Manny, this is a toe," I said. "And it works on butts."

I booted the ball, a toe-basher, at full speed into the net, shearing an inch of fright off poor Dolt's crop.

"That, boys, is what you call a goal. Do any of you recognize it?"

Sarcasm was a play for all ages, and it hurt. And they would hurt more.

"Do you want to feel what it is like to score a goal in soccer or are you going to be known as the only team in soccer history that never scored a goal, not one time?"

Some lips began to tremble. SOS signals were flashed to the sidelines but we were too far away for the *Carpathia* to come to the rescue of the *Titanic*. We were going down, the captain of the ship was missing, and the first officer was rearranging the deck chairs.

"We are going to have a penalty kick competition," I said. "One thing is for sure. You will leave this season knowing what it feels like to score a goal, even if it is only here today at training. I'm going to show you what a goal looks like from the goalie's perspective. We don't need Dolt today. He already knows what it feels like to pick the ball out of the net. So, I am going to take a penalty kick against each and every one of you. I want you to feel the wind as the ball flies past you, and I want you to think: I like that noise. I want to make that noise, too."

They went in goal one by one. I battered the ball as hard as I could, making sure I missed hitting them square on the forehead, as that kind of behavior was criminal. The players winced, dived out the way, while some stood gaping, staring straight ahead. One at a time, they picked the ball out of the net and walked it back to me. I leaned over them and whispered into their ears, "That's what you call a goal. Remember it."

Now it was their turn. There would be no goalkeeper. The ball was placed on the penalty spot, a mere twelve yards away. Manny stepped up first. He missed, blasting it wide. Speedy Gonzalez, in a gesture of ironic praise to his accelerated personality, rolled the ball into the net in slow motion, then raised his hands in the scoring gesture and sped off across the field, zooming madly in zany zigzags.

The potted plant simply stood at the ball and waited.

"Kick it!" I screamed.

He ran away.

"He's crying," said Manny. "You made him cry."

"Good. It's in my coaching manual."

The practice ended. Mahmoud was missing. I was probably the next to disappear.

CHAPTER 15

Cursed

A few days later, I pulled on the Dockers and the loafers, and suited up for another outing as assistant coach to the foul-breathed Dragons.

But as soon as I stepped onto the balding scrap of grass that the league called a soccer field, I saw some of the parents approaching me at speed, as if they were a mechanized division of the Afrika Korps. I was quickly surrounded. They looked like they were in lynching mood. Lawsuits, disbarment from coaching, shame and blame, all of it flashed through my condemned man thoughts. I dropped like a stone into an involuntary deep knee bend.

"You pick the team," they said. "Mahmoud is gone. You are the head coach now."

And with that, I fell over.

I had no choice but to assume the mantle of destiny, to lead my gladiators into the little league Coliseum. Mahmoud was history. The disappearance curse had worked.

All the titles of power filled my mind. Kommandant, King,

President, Emperor, General Secretary, CEO, Field Marshal, Kaiser Permanente. The revolution could now begin. La Grande Terreur would open the veins and the Dragons would fly, getting off the ground at last, and we would burn loss from our efforts with fiery blasts of goals, the enemy's nets reduced to cinders, our dominance arching in the sky, free from our chain in the dungeon and other poetic hyperbolic mince.

The parents would know how it was to feel victorious. I would be the deliverer. They would think: He's a man who can lead. He's a man who could fix the potholes in my street. I'll vote for that guy!

All mad dictators needed a right-hand man. And on cue, the shapeless form of a dwarf with historical crags welded onto his shortened stature stepped forward to offer himself as assistant coach.

The father of our Kurdish Speedy Gonzalez was now to fulfill his destiny, too. This was no surprise. I had noticed him laying out cones at previous practices, trying to curry favor with Mahmoud. I looked down upon him. His hair, which had once resembled barbed wire stretching across the front lines of defeated history, had been oddly transformed into a thin welcome mat of slimy dandruff. He was head and shoulders below the rest of us.

Like the Scots, the Kurds walked through history's valley sharing someone else's clothes. Kurds had had to adorn the hats of several nations to stay alive. Hated by nationalist Turks and disfigured by Sunni Arab scumbags like Saddam, Kurds found their hearths in constant danger of being snuffed out. They had no national soccer team, no thriving leagues, and no soccer giants. The original team photo of the Dragons would be sent for redevelopment to USSR laboratories, where Mahmoud's treacherous face would be made to disappear, to be replaced by the Kurd, the new *l'homme a droit.*

"Coaching the Dragons is a high bar," I told him. He was unlikely to win any high jump competition in any sporting future so there was no danger of a putsch against me.

"You're the assistant," I said.

So the sons of Saladin were joining up with the holy cross of St. Andrew. Who knew? Maybe a thousand years ago a Scottish crusading knight had met up with a Kurd outside the gates of Jerusalem and they said to each other: "In a thousand years, there will be a nation of power built on donuts and endless blue sky, and we'll meet again in this place of dreams to fulfill the hopes of children, beyond the fractures of the Prophet and Jesus, beyond the burning of the churches, the molestation of the mosques, the sacking of the synagogue, and the trials of the temple. Be not cold, brother Kurd, brother Scot, by a lack of freedom in your lands but be warmed by the folds of men."

Kurdistan and Scotland: destined to be friends. We had a shared sense of misery. His son was no longer a Mexican cartoon mouse. His son was a vein from the heart of nations longing for freedom. The Kurd was my ally and I was glad to see that Dockers were now making a size for him.

"What's it like in Kurdistan?" I asked him.

"Kurdistan? What's that? I'm Italian," he said.

"Mahmoud told me you were a Kurd!"

His face harrumphed and he took on the look of a midget Il Duce, with a bad hair transplant.

All that time wasted thinking about fucking Kurdistan's plight, and all that shite about shared loss, and feelings of sympathy for what turned out to be an Italian with a dodgy *duomo*.

Fuck Mahmoud and fuck Saladin and all the fucking salad bars that came after them, I thought.

So it was Italy. The land of olive oil, and for so long stirring the world with art and wonders and . . . Oh, shut up!

* * * *

At my first full training session in charge, I sent Il Duce off to mark out the perimeter with bright flashy cones, the sanctuary into which no parent could set foot without my permission. I brought forth the power of curses to the team.

"Okay, listen. I'm in charge now. You will call me Coach. The last game was the worst performance ever. It was a disgrace to soccer. Why did you all chase the dog that ran on the field when you should have been chasing the ball? We must end this curse, this jinx! No more! I'm going to teach you all how to tackle today, and I want to see you take what you learn and apply it in our next game. Do you understand me? We have to get the ball off the other team. The secret of a crunching tackle is to commit the crime and leave no evidence. And then you invade your enemy's territory with the ball at your feet and take everything from them."

"Like the computer game Age of Empires," said Manny.

"Exactly. Like Age of Empires."

"I like killing the villagers," he said.

"I like building walls to keep out the enemy," said the Dolt in Need of a Volt.

Lord save us.

I went on, "Well, try doing that on Saturday. Some of you know my coaching philosophy already. Now the rest of you will hear it. *Get stuck in!* We are only going to win games if we can be tough guys and make the other team fear us. Up until now we have been a bunch of weaklings. But now we're over that. The problem has disappeared. And it's time for us to put the curse on the other foot. The other team."

Il Duce came into earshot.

"So we're playing for fun and since our little penalty competition we've been scoring goals in training and now we're going to score lots of goals in the games. It's Santa Claus time. Lots of goals in Santa's bag are coming down the chimney."

"I don't believe in Santa," said Manny.

"We don't celebrate Christmas in my house," said a kid with blond curls.

(Who was he? Had I seen him before?)

"I don't care if you believe in Santa or not. I want a bag of goals from you. That's your present to me!"

"I believe in Santa," said the prehistoric fern.

It was time for the talk to be over—I ran them ragged. I barked orders like Caesar commanding the legions in Gaul. By the end of the practice, the Dragons were gasping for breath. Some seemed close to fainting. The new imperious regime was off to an excellent, if brutal, start. There would be more to come. I would make warriors of them before the campaign came to an end. The coaching philosophy of "getting stuck in" was about to be taken to a new level.

Game day. I arrived at the field early to survey the battleground. The language of massacre popped into my head. It was soccer's lexicon. "We'll slaughter them on Saturday," or "We'll wipe those bastards out." I had heard it many times at soccer games. "Shut them down," yelled supporters as if they were government censors. "Take no prisoners," was another breach of the Geneva Conventions happily employed. When nations played soccer against each other, the rival press corps splattered ink calling for Crusades and Deliverance, Strength and Will.

The troughs and holes on the playing field were First World War material.

"What a fucking disgrace," I said to a poor sod painting lines. "This field is an insult to soccer. What's the meaning of this?"

"You should see the fields up the road. Dog shit, glass; someone said they found needles there," he said.

"What?"

"Yeah. Can you believe it?"

"It wouldn't be that if it were a baseball diamond. The city would be down there to make it sparkle."

"Hey, what's your team? Are you a coach?"

"Yes. Head coach. Dragons. We burn people."

Il Duce was standing at the side of the field with his arms folded, nodding. Speedy Gonzalez was bombing around the holes in the park chasing the ball as if it were a roll of Cheddar. The other players began to drift in. And there across the way were today's enemy and their supporters.

Supporters!

What the fuck? Besides parents, they had fans. That was something new! And they had a banner with the team's name on it. They had a soccer chant. It reverberated around the ground. Real soccer fans! And included in their starting eleven were many child dwarves. Had Il Duce been fathering away from home?

I walked over to their coach to do the introduction and the silent "you lose" curse. I noticed that one of their dwarves had a hearing aid. Was that allowed under FIFA rules? I assumed it was a hearing aid. Maybe it was a device that received messages from the sidelines.

I sought out the referee who was checking the nets.

"Hey, Ref. Head Coach Black with the Dragons. One of their squad is wearing some kind of ear device. I know that we can't wear jewelry and earrings, which is an inconvenience for my diamond team, but is it allowed under the rules that a player can wear an electronic device in his ear?"

"He's deaf," said the ref.

"Excuse me?"

"He's deaf."

"So what? It might be a hazard. Can't they use hand signals?"

"It's little league."

"No, Ref. It's soccer."

I turned and marched with a slight goosestep to my team.

I gathered them together.

"We're playing against a set of deaf dwarves from *Lord of the Rings* today."

"I love *Lord of the Rings*," said Manny.

"I love Aragorn," said the Dolt.

"No. Gollum is so, so cool with his evil powers—"

"Be quiet!" I yelled, like a pissed Gandalf. "This is our fellowship of the Ring. We are the dragon's breath and we'll slaughter those dwarves out there today."

"But the dwarves were on our side in the movie," said the potted plant.

"What?"

"The dwarves are our friends in *Lord of the Rings*," he said.

"I don't give a hoot! They're cursed now! They've been turned evil by the bad guy . . . what's his name, Solomon or something like that . . . but it doesn't matter. Listen. We're here to get stuck into them. I want you to leave a mark on the dwarves."

"Like the dwarves in *Snow White*," said Manny.

"Like bloody *Snow White*!" I said.

"What's 'bloody' mean?" said the Dolt.

Il Duce was over talking to the parents. I saw his lips move but at this distance I couldn't make out the exact words. If I thought for one minute that he was saying anything bad about me, he'd wake up tomorrow a foot shorter. I was on a roll. All it would take was a silent recitation of the "foot shorter" curse.

I looked at the opponents and their diminutive setup.

"Come on," I screamed to the Dragons. "Fly over and roast them!"

Il Duce took up his place next to me on the sideline. The parents seemed excited about the prospects for today's game. They came right up to the edge of the field. I could hear the supporters for the Dwarves on the other side of the field singing a song.

The referee expelled and the pea battered itself inside the plastic casing. I pulled off my wedding ring and put it in my pocket. I thought of the vanishing Mahmoud.

My kid was standing next to me.

"When can I go on?" he said.

"We have to be fair. Everyone gets a chance to play."

The game moved off and fans could pick up a copy of the *Sporting Green* to find out how the new imperial regime had fared in its first battle in what might be called the Puny Wars.

THE SPORTING GREEN

DWARVES HAMMER WEAK DRAGONS

The new head coach of the Dragons used so many vile oaths and curses at his prematch press conference that this newspaper would run the risk of lawsuits should it publish the comments of this increasingly unstable goon. And televisions channels could not show the postmatch press conference for fear of huge fines from the FCC. And in between the pre- and postmatch press conferences, Coach Black's team was crushed by a set of diminutives playing at a higher level of soccer.

The tendentious "get stuck in" coaching philosophy, not easily translated from its primitive Scottish origin, suddenly makes sense today. The Dragons are "stuck in" the mud and the season is still sinking. With Scotty now at the helm of the enterprise, all we can expect is flurries of irrational gestures marked by the reality of the laws of physics. "We're going down, Captain."

The Dragons attempted to harvest legs on Saturday, hoping to build on their violent display in the previous game. But the tiny boys were darting around their scything legs, running through their back four, chipping the ball over the Dolt in Need of a Million Volts, and speeding through on goal to score again and again and again and again.

Coach Black's erratic sideline behavior continued with insane, turbinelike arm waving. He trolled a new ditch of embarrassment for his team. Hoping to generate enough wind with his windmill action to propel the ball away from his defenders, he only succeeded in nearly taking the head off his diminutive assistant, the insensitively nicknamed Il Duce.

At the postmatch press conference, Coach Black was asked if his windmill arms indicated a new coaching style. Readers should note that the expletives have been removed.

"Yes, it is. And it works. The people coach Tony Robbins, who has managed to windmill his way into a windfall of dollars, has influenced me. I am hoping that I will be able to generate a windfall of goals for the Dragons. It may take some time. You can't convert your energy to a new source overnight. It may take a few weeks but the benefits to the Dragons will be profound. It's very environmental, using wind as a motivator."

On a neutral note, today's game was something quite special. It felt as if it were being played inside a stadium. The Dwarves brought a strong traveling support to the match. Their fans' songs and chants echoed off the amphitheater of trees that surrounded the field. It was a welcome reminder that soccer is a game that requires more than a park, a ball, and players. It requires loud and colorful supporters, songs and wild cheers, and the occasional riot.

CHAPTER 16

Hooligans

heerleaders would have been nice. The high kicks and pom-poms, the miniskirts and flashes: D-r-a-g-o-n-s! They would form a gauntlet and the head coach would stroll through as they went wild. I found a Christian cheerleaders group on the Internet but they wore chastity belts under their skirts and stood perfectly still when they rah-rah-rahed.

I fantasized about going a step further than just plain fans and whoopy girls. It would be unique to have a hooligan crew, the first such offering in American little league soccer history.

Born would be the SMC—the Soccer Mom Crew, to give it a cool hooligan moniker. They would be the most feared gang of suburbanite hooligans imaginable. The SMC would need money and plenty of spare time. They would require cover, a blend to meld into after decimating the enemy with their riotous acts. An appreciation of wardrobe was essential, as hooligans enjoyed wearing the finest labels. A gathering place would be needed, an American version of a dangerous

English soccer hooligan pub. Starbucks. It had to be good for something. The soccer hooligan movement of America would be born from the frothy Frappuccino and they would be big tough vaginas. This gang of deranged soccer moms would plan their attacks on your Starbucks and burn your fucking malls to the ground.

Once a week, before the game, they would gather to plan the attack. Pamela would buy the fair trade coffee, Jennifer would secure the baked good nibbles, and Jane would bring the weed and Valium for the post-riot party. The Starbucks coffee would be swallowed for free, thanks to threats against the staff, and the SMC would thank Starbucks, the corporate sponsor, in all its future commercial engagements including its HBO series, *Hooligan Mom*. SMC tattoos would adorn ankles, the design a paper coffee cup with the SMC letters rising like steam. The hooligan moms would squeeze each other in loving embrace and touch each other's sharpened haircuts.

Feel this point on this new cut. This will stab the eyes of those fat slobs on Saturday.

And they would be gorgeous and deadly, the SMC and their Munch-a-Mocha!

I'm going to slash that bitch's tires on her van. She's going to be wearing *that Frappuccino she carries around with her! There will be no Pilates for her for a while.*

Soon, the entire land would be terrified of the SMC. The FBI would open a file. Anderson Cooper at CNN would do a Special Investigation, and have his silver head kicked in by the SMC, his whiny voice begging for mercy as stilettos punctured his perfect balls. No critic in the country would be safe. And the SMC would strike like assassins. The SMC's SUVs and family wagons would be undetectable by the authorities. And left on the battered torsos of their victims, the smell of SMC perfume. No amount of showering could ever remove that fragrance. Once you met the SMC, it was for life.

● ● ● ●

At training practice, I conferred with my Roman assistant.

"This idea of training is a myth. Training for what? Training for another whipping?" I said.

"I think we need to rearrange the team, try and mix up the positions, play the attackers in defense, make the defenders the attackers," suggested Il Duce.

No wonder Italy lost the war.

"Well, I'll consider your advice. I want the players to be tougher. You know my philosophy. We have to learn to fight before we can win. How many times have I said it?"

"Like the Ultras."

"What?"

"We have to learn to fight like the Ultras."

The Ultras were Italy's most dangerous violent soccer criminals—they fought, and threw Nazi salutes, and generally set fire to things like stadiums and other fans.

"Exactly. Like the Ultras."

"These boys don't know anything like that. It's not in their culture," he said.

"If only we could take them on a field trip and teach them how to be riotous, we'd win some games."

Another violent fantasy! Imagine a mini gang of horrible little Dragon thugs on the rampage, Les Affreux. We would take the bus to GapKids, dodge paying the fare and tell the driver to drive or die, then, once at the store, eleven kids would rattle the windows, flick boogers, march into the shop, and find the droopy-eyed guy folding the jeans for the hundredth time that hour and say,

"Hey, Denim Boy! Sort us out with the top jeans."

While he was running around panicked, following requests and barks, some of the Dragons would be stuffing their duffel bags with free shirts, sweaters, and those cute little colored socks. When it was time to pay, Denim Boy would be tied up with his hipster belt and have an old sock stuffed in his mouth.

"Say thank you," I would yell. "Remember your manners."

"Thank you! Thanks! 'Bye! Sorry. I hope you'll be okay."

Next stop, the ice cream shop, leaning over the counter, sticking their little fingers into the chocolate chip cookie flavor, smashing cones in faces, taunting the patrons and chanting *Dragons are we! Dragons are we!*

Then the sirens would come. The boys in blue would run in with Tasers blazing, guns out, yelling, "Where are the TV cameras?"

And all they would find would be angels with ice cream faces.

"The SMC did it, Officer. They went that way."

And off the cops would run. Sirens fading.

But Il Duce was right. These American kids would never possess the European spirit of the hooligan psycho and know what it was like to be snared in a soccer riot.

I did. I had been caught up in a few as a kid. Old men pushed young men to the ground, frightened dads grabbed their boys, and scabrous oaths and curses went up as if they could shield people from barrages of bottles and piss-filled beer cans. After the riot, you could see the sexy beer cans lying in the gutter—Scottish brewers adorned them with images of scantily clad female models, an advertising ploy in the days before sexist guilt. There was piss and foam leaking out of their openings.

And once, I nearly died. My brother and I had gone to a big game at the national stadium. It was a gorgeous day, hot, which was rare enough. We were dehydrating. Milk-colored male torsos were exposed to the sun for the first time in years. They were turning a little sour. Beer splashed over the crowd; it was the Scottish version of sunscreen. There was nothing to eat, no concession stands, so empty stomachs had been filled to the brim with lager.

After the game, outside the stadium, we started running from a swilling mob armed with beer cans transformed into weapons of piss destruction. Like a herd of beast hoofing it across the plains, feet pounded the road, and dust rose in the air. A gauntlet of buildings slammed upward to the sky, right and left. There was no escape. Hundreds were now running at full speed down a funnel of fear. Smashing bottles started to land in the ranks at the rear. I grabbed my brother's hand—he was only ten years old, three years younger than me. The crowd swept us along, until suddenly a man coming in the opposite direction grabbed my neck and screamed, "Stand your fucking ground!"

Up ahead, hundreds were racing toward us, and hundreds were behind us, chasing the racers. The trap snapped shut. My brother's hand slipped from mine.

He was gone.

The battle was now upon me. Tears swam down my face. Where was he? I tried to go back for him, into the riot, but I was flattened by the mob. Feet pounded over me; people tripped and fell. A boot kicked me in the side. Suddenly, a man grabbed me by the collar and yanked me up, dragging me with him to the sidewalk, slapping a few hooligans on the way. He left me in a doorway and then charged back into the fray. But where was my brother?

And then I saw him, standing in a doorway farther down.

"Fucking mental," he said as I ran up, in tears.

CHAPTER 17

Moms

In Scotland, most boys first met the world of soccer alongside their dads. "Father and son at the match" was the way we men bonded. In the old days, clubs allowed boys to watch games for free. Dads lifted their sons over the turnstile at the stadium. It was a magic moment, you felt quite special. You knew then that you belonged to something bigger. During the match you would look up and feel bad as your dad grimaced as your team conceded a goal, or maybe you would catch him in a moment of unbridled ecstasy as the final whistle blew and you'd scored a magnificent victory.

My dad hated soccer. He didn't do any of that for me.

. . . .

For a start he was born with two left feet, and to make matters worse, he had chosen the career of cop. On game day, he spent a lot of his time arresting violent soccer fans, or avoiding missiles being thrown at his head by hooligans.

"Get that blasted ball out of my sight," he'd say, as my

brother and I wrecked the living room with our version of indoor soccer.

My love of the game came from my mum. Often, on bleak winter days, she would bundle us up in scarves and gloves and escort us to a small local soccer stadium, lifting us over the turnstile and leaving us to it. We never doubted that she would be waiting for us at the exit following the final whistle. As the other boys headed home with their dads, my mum would be listening to our gripes and moans about referees and missed open goals, nodding her head in sympathy. It wasn't just during the World Cup that she'd stand in the living room doing the ironing, throwing lobs of disquiet at the action on the TV; she'd watch any game. But when Scotland did play, there was always a guaranteed laugh to be had, an own goal maybe, or a dreadful goalkeeping blunder, and my mum would rip her sides as the comedy of errors unfolded on the screen. But she didn't just laugh at them—she was a maestro when it came to the controlled oath, verbally burning crap players as if she was ironing their shirts as they wore them. That said, she was loyal to the country. Naturally, she booed the English national anthem when it was played at Scotland games by loyalist bagpipe bands. She didn't like it much when England won a game, either. She taught me that lesson. Whenever England played, you hoped the other team would win.

My mum took a dim view of her neighbors who complained about us kicking the ball over the hedge and in their gardens, or slamming it against a window.

"Where else will the boys play?" she asked of a childless couple that lived next door.

She was also a shrewd businesswoman, a kind of George Steinbrenner for my section of Glasgow. Salary caps and luxury tax be damned—she gave me the fivepence trade money to buy our rival's best player, a boy called Carnwath, the owner of a shot that could blow holes in castle walls. That dime was the biggest transfer fee ever paid in boys' soccer in my neighborhood. And it was a shrewd investment, as our results against local opponents improved, giving me cause to thank my mum and obediently eat my vegetables. I wasn't a wee man, because Mum had bought Carnwath.

Mum attended only one professional game, but being a wheeler and dealer she somehow made it onto the TV. Watching the television highlights later that night, I caught a glimpse of her sitting in her seat close to the field. Her face was a picture of glee.

I suppose things weren't that different here. The sidelines at Dragons games were jammed with soccer moms. Soccer was the mother of all sports. It was refreshing. Women loved soccer for more profound reasons than men. The field was a big womb and their babies were in there kicking. The umbilical cords were still attached and down the pipe came urgent feeds of advice. Little boys turned and looked to their moms for that vital emotional support, affirming everything was going to work out fine. And when defeat and hurt struck, mom would rush forward with her protective cloak and spur Junior to dust himself off; she'd wipe tears from his little cheeks and hold him tight until he was strong again to face the troubles of a cruel world. Great loyalty was born from soccer, moms and their lads. It was a match made in heaven.

One evening, the Fern's mom came up to me at practice and said, "Your coaching is not producing any improvement in our results."

I admired her straightforward hack.

"I'm not to blame," I explained. "Mahmoud is. He never instilled a will to win in the players. I guess you can understand it, him being Iranian and all."

"What's that got to do with it?" she said.

"They're rubbish at soccer."

"And Scotland isn't?" she said.

"Listen, things are going to improve, now that we have Scotland and Italy in control. Give me more time to leave my mark."

The look on her face said it all.

"When was the last time you played soccer? Have you ever played soccer?"

"Yes, of course I have," I said, wounded. "In fact, my final game of competitive soccer was against ladies."

It could never have happened in Scotland when I was growing up. Women did not play soccer, period, amen. They played netball (a form of basketball but without the dribbling, dunking, fast breaks, or any real excitement whatsoever) or field hockey, this in little short skirts that flew up in gusts. It was different in America, of course. Team USA had won the World Cup. Brandi Chastain took her kit off at the end of the game. This meant that she was strong *and* sexy. There had even been a brief women's league, but no one bothered to watch it.

Coed soccer was all the rage at amateur level, too. Pretty much every urban area had a vibrant coed league. As for me, by the early nineties, my knees were gathering gristle and making sounds like the Tin Man's joints in *The Wizard of Oz*. Nevertheless, a friend had forced me to join his coed team. Pulling on my boots, I thought to myself, *This shouldn't be too hard, playing against a bunch of girls.*

And there I was, sprinting onto the field for my first game since moving to the States. Winded, I pulled back a bit, and went through a series of strenuous twists and turns, mimicking the exercises the professionals performed while warming up. Pulling players to me in a circle, I proffered my sage advice to the girls.

One of them spat on the ground.

Ignoring her, I announced, "You guys will soon be on the winning track." I think I may have even believed it.

• • • •

The game commenced. My marker was a woman with a short haircut adorned with colored spikes that looked like rosebuds.

"Can I call you Rose?" I asked her. She blanked me.

I liked the look of this. I felt cocky. I couldn't wait to slide the ball through her legs, tickle her fancy with some nimble toe work, and wait for a crack in her defense before I slotted home.

"*AAAAARGH!* Fuck me! What was that?" I shouted, finding myself flat on my back, a bulletlike pain coursing through my right ankle. Rose was standing over me. The ball had long since gone back toward where it had come from.

"Get up and don't whine, you pussy," she said, stomping on my foot as she ran away. Within two minutes of that assault, she with the big boots had clobbered me again, only this time her knee had drilled deep into my colon, sending a rip of pain through every vertebra.

"Fer fuck sake, Referee!" I yelled.

The referee pretended to ignore me, desperately trying to keep up with the game as she was.

So this game was to be war between the sexes.

"You fucking Irish asshole," said Rose, picking me up roughly. I didn't think it would be appropriate to correct her on a minor geographical point.

Thankfully, the halftime whistle blew. I spoke to my team captain.

"I'm injured. I need my legs. I'm a bartender."

"No, you're not injured," she said. "You're just scared of that woman who's marking you."

I saw Rose across the way, gargling Gatorade and spitting it out in a gush of violent intent. What kind of nut job was she?

"She's a florist," said one of my teammates.

"And I'm the stalk she's cutting down."

I stood waiting for the whistle to start the second half. I could see Rose's red strip down the field. I revved my foot like a bull in the ring. She would not be beating me up anymore.

I waited for her to get the ball. Now was my chance to get some revenge. I stormed forward but she raised her elbow and sent me flying in the direction from whence I had come. The referee saw the incident and reached for her red card.

"About time, Referee," I said, and then to my total disbelief, I realized that I was the one heading for the showers.

"You can't be serious!" I said, but there was no recourse.

My team slaughtered me with derision as I hung my head in shame and limped off.

After the game, reflecting on my bruises in the pub's toilet mirror, and having a hard time getting anyone to buy me a beer, I realized one of the truths about soccer. Success in the game had nothing to do with being a boy or a girl. Having big feet attached to the end of a violent personality was what you needed, if you were a little short of talent, as Rose so clearly was. My soccer career had ended in ignominious humiliation. I took my boots home and hung them up in the closet, where they dried and rotted like the flowers of forgotten glory.

CHAPTER 18

Atmosphere

After such a violent end to my career, I received a heartening reminder of the softer side of the universe: a care package from my mom in Scotland.

Three bars of Yorkies

Four tubes of Smarties

Two boxes of PG Tips tea

A packet of Orange Clubs

A packet of Bisto for mince and tatties

One box of Mr. Kipling Apple Pies

Six Mars Bars

Two Flakes

A box of Tunnock's Mallows (only available in Scotland)

A jar of marmalade

A tin of haggis

McCain's Oven Chips

A copy of *Private Eye*

A news article from the *Rutherglen Reformer,* a small Glasgow newspaper

The article was about Shawfield, the local stadium where I watched professional soccer as a kid. This was the place where I had learned the importance of the word "atmosphere" when it came to the soccer experience. And it was a place where they served up death.

Clyde Football Club played at Shawfield. They were a minor league team, perennially rubbish. But I supported Clyde; still do. The atmosphere in Shawfield was like the atmosphere on Pluto. Exposure was a real and constant worry for the fans. Frostbite not unheard of. The sun never shined.

Like tiny flowers at the top of the Rocky Mountains, the weeds on the terracing steps at Shawfield had developed immunity to subzero weather conditions and annihilation. Holes had appeared in the corrugated roof, and echoes mastered the void. At every game, I stood isolated in a stadium built for twenty-five thousand people. The nearest fan to me was one hundred yards to my right or left. The older boosters would tell me about matches in the 1950s when the place was alight with noise, packed with bodies. By the time I was a ticket buyer in the 1970s, there was no fear of being stomped to death, no multitudes roaring for the team. By then, five hundred paying patrons was considered a decent crowd. It was sporting fandom at the coalface of utter decay. Being a Clyde fan was like being part of a dissident minority banished to a sporting Siberia.

Desperate to create an exciting aura, an amateur hobbyist who had an aptitude for sound experimentation turned up at the stadium on game day determined to deliver a big-game atmosphere to the players and the Clyde fans. He had a seventies boom box attached to a megaphone. On the cassette inside the device was a recording of crowd cheers sampled from television coverage of popular, big crowd soccer games. He pressed Play. The agonizing nails-down-a-blackboard feedback from the megaphone snapped the tips off the icicles hanging from the corrugated roof. The spinal cords of the players froze. Folks covered their ears. The two policemen on duty moved in quickly and removed the sonic hooligan device. Haunting echoes faded and returned the Clyde experience to a barren Sea of Tranquility.

And then there was death. To keep the few fans warm and fed at Shawfield, the club operated, near the toilets, a food hatch where old men in flower aprons sold two nourishing products that contributed to Glasgow males having an average lifespan of 63.7 years: the Scotch meat pie and the cup of hot Bovril.

A cup of Bovril beef stock resembled something brown and smelled like something brown. It was consumed in large volumes, helping to wash the Scotch meat pie into the intestinal maze and around any rapidly growing bowel obstacles. This horrendous double act of dietary danger knew no greater performers. As powerful as any pharmaceutical laxatives, the antiquated plumbing system at Shawfield was stretched to the limits, disintegrating with a vile ugliness to which the dryness of words could in no way do justice. Fortunately for the stadium plumbing, the pipes had only to run a short distance to Glasgow's River Clyde, the inspiration for our club name. Back then, the great shipbuilding river was dark rusted water filled with iron filings, amputated ship parts, and meat pie and Bovril deposits sailing down the river on a Saturday afternoon. Some people went fishing in the Clyde, hoping to hook cast-off shoes or wallets from those who jumped in, the suicides unable to weather the Glasgow diet any longer.

Mad cow disease had not been invented back then but it was soon to be on the Scottish menu. As the catatonic started to pile up in the 1980s and 1990s, scientists discovered that products like the Scotch meat pie, a delicacy made from chopped-up low-grade cow that had been fed the spinal cords and brains of their fellows, was likely a source of contamination. Fortunately, I never ate the pies. I stood well away from the clutch of fans that hovered near the hatch.

I looked to the bottom of the parcel from Mom in Scotland. There was one item I had missed. It was a jar of Bovril.

"Excellent," I said, "I'll feed this to the Dragons. This will get their asses in gear."

Dear Reverend Murray,

As I write this letter to you, I am drinking a warm cup of beef stock known as Bovril. It comes from Scotland and it is not a drink that makes you drunk. I recommend it to you if you have any problems with constipation, which I know is a hidden ailment for many in the church.

I wanted you to know that I am doing the work of the Lord out here in California by trying to save my lawn.

My lawn is ill, sir. It needs prayer. Evil black weeds turfed out the green. But I am planning on saving it from this abortionist evil. I have launched Operation Lawn Rescue. Americans! Save your lawns! It is our patriotic duty to keep our lawns virgin, to take a stand against neglect, to stop the spread of weed seed. When the Lord returns he will want to see nice green grass outside our suburban homes. He will not be happy if he has to bring a gardener with him. I have not had much luck in getting you to read out my letters on the air but maybe you could answer this question for me: Does God employ illegal aliens to do the gardens in heaven?

Yours faithfully,
Alan Black

A friend called me.

"You're not still coaching that soccer team, are you?"

"Of course I am. I'm the head coach now. I'm turning it around."

"What happened to the other guy, the Iranian?"

"He's gone missing."

"That sounds suspicious. Hey, listen. I have a couple of tickets for Giants baseball. Fancy it?"

"Yeah, I could do with some healing from this soccer trauma. It's been ages since I went to a stadium. I need the atmosphere. It might lift my spirits."

I sat listening to the soporific organ used to sedate the fans. Hearing it, they clapped along like robots and mildly cheered at the crescendo. I suspected the organ playing at baseball games was invented at a weekend CIA Officers Retreat when the mind control division came across the idea while singing hymns at the church service on the Sunday morning.

Soon, sellers arrived with candy floss flopping in the wind, with huge genetically modified pretzels, and with ice cream.

"I can't get away from you two," I said to Ben and Jerry, as I rose to my feet to watch another Barry Bonds homer sink into San Francisco Bay. Now that the crowd had its fix and were satisfied that the price of the ticket was not entirely unreasonable, they all returned to what they did best at baseball games: talking on their cell phones and eating.

The guy next to me was scoring the game. This I appreciated. He was a real fan. He paid rapt attention to every ball, strike, and play. His ear was plugged into a transistor radio, too, listening to the game commentary. At one point I asked him how the scoring worked, and he completely ignored me. I liked that.

For the rest of the fans, the public announcer with the horrible voice kept us informed of who was up and who was out. Baseball was about sitting on your ass. Besides a home run or a trip to the head or an excursion for a food-beer double, the only time fans got up was for the seventh-inning stretch. It was the only exercise a lot of these people would get all year. But still I drank the weak beer, ate the warm ice cream. Eventually nature took its course and I went to the toilet to escape the boredom. But even there a speaker broadcast the commentary.

"Change up. I knew he was going to throw that one," said the sportscaster, expert after the fact. Commentators were the same in every sport.

I returned to my plastic seat to the accompaniment of the soundtrack on the public address system. It kicked in during a pitching change. "Blitzkreig Bop" by the Ramones. I guess the lyrical link for the departing pitcher was "Shoot him in the back now," which made sense in gun-mad America.

I said to my friend, "They should be singing 'Beat on the brat with a baseball bat.'"

And where was the spontaneity of fan singing in American sports? For a country that had invented Motown and rock and roll, you would have thought singing at the stadium would be a part of sports fan culture. But again, they needed prompting. They would sing along to the soundtrack mixed by the stadium DJ. I had heard strapping baseball-capped men in San Francisco harmonize with Freddie Mercury in "We Are the Champions" while holding their six-inch dogs in their favorite hand. The Beach Boys' "California Girls" was another join-in classic that appealed to men and lesbians around the Golden Gate. But at the top of the sports arena hit parade for many years was the anthem penned by the great British pedophile Gary Glitter. *Rock and ro-oll. Hey! Rock and roll,* with its big slam, was sung across the nation, at stadiums and arenas in places like Arkansas, Texas, and Oklahoma, states where podiatrists listed themselves as foot doctors to avoid any confusion.

In Scottish stadiums, soccer fan songs were pure opera, rich and deep, revealing tales of prejudice, suspicion, disgrace, and humiliation. We sang about everything—other teams, other players, other towns, other ways of life—anything, in short, that wasn't us and ours and what we knew. A good example was this ditty, written by Celtic fans and sung to the tune of the Scout Camp classic, "The Quartermaster's Store." It was dedicated to a Rangers player named Ian Durrant.

He's gay, he's bent, his ass is up for rent.
Ian Durrant! Ian Durrant!
He's gay, he's bent, his ass is up for rent.
Ian Durrant! Ian Durrant!

It goes on still. Manchester United has a player called Park—he's from Korea. He's a big fan favorite. And this is what they sing—to the old American Shaker tune "Simple Gifts"—about their own player:

Park, Park, wherever you may be
You eat dogs in your own country
But it could be worse, you could be a fucking Scouse [a person
from Liverpool]
Eating rats in your council house.

Pleasant stuff. Back at the San Francisco Giants, the hand-clapping machine came over the public address system. The programmed fans joined in. I was sick of being led by the nose. So I tried on my own to create an atmosphere, on my day out to the stadium. I threw goobers off the top deck down into the more expensive seats where the wealthy sat chatting about the market and occasionally looking up to see who the fuck was throwing goobers at them. And I sang a song to the tune of Boney M's "Brown Girl in the Ring."

Barry Bonds is on the dope
La-la-la-la-la
Barry Bonds is on the dope
La, la-la-la-la-la
Barry Bonds is on the dope
La-la-la-la-la
His balls have shriveled like a plum.
Plum. Plum.

The zombies immediately around me were not impressed. Neither was my pal.

"Shut up, you Scottish ignoramus," he said. "You're only supposed to sing 'Take Me Out to the Ball Game' and the national anthem, nu soul style."

More bored than ever, I headed to concessions and stuffed myself with dogs and wondered why Poland had attached itself to junk food.

"Maybe Bonds ate this stuff," I told my friend as my stomach bloated up.

CHAPTER 19

Injuries

The night before game 8, I was at work. The bar I work in is a Scottish-themed establishment owned by a Korean family. This made perfect sense. Koreans drank a lot, yelled at each other, acted moody, and had seen their homelands trampled by a neighboring asshole country. Their language had been suppressed, their culture assaulted. They were the Scotland of Asia. And, they loved soccer.

The bar served newspaper-wrapped fish and chips from a Korean-owned store conveniently located around the corner. It was just like home. I had grown up eating fish and chips several times a week, sometimes several times a day. The stuff we serve at the bar is cooked in a real fish fryer, imported from Britain, and they come slathered in tons of tasty salt and vinegar. People flock to the pub for the experience. Once, an XXL-sized customer who had wolfed down the meal noticed that his fish supper had come wrapped in the obituary section of the newspaper.

We never saw him again.

It was tough work, making this tasty food. The boiling oil

from the fryer would spatter the Koreans' arms and hands, leaving wisps of tiny scars. Faces were slimed by it, too, and had to be hard scrubbed after each shift. Because of how hard the job was, drinking on the job was essential, and the pub supplied the poor bastards with Heineken, all night long.

Finally, one of them snapped. The headline on one of the greasy newspapers could have read: TRADITIONAL SCOTTISH FOOD MURDERED BY KOREAN LUNATIC.

He killed a fish supper. On the night of the crime, besides slaving at the fryer, he was delivering the food to the bar, too, carrying the fish and chips down an alleyway littered with homeless people in wheelchairs, some of them missing a limb or two. Midget hookers blew creeps in the doorways, transsexual whores flashed what they shouldn't have, and abandoned crack pipes and needles lay everywhere.

Into this hell came the drunk Korean. Maybe a starving hand reaching out for a chip had accosted him. Or perhaps he had been offered relief at the gummy heights of the midget hooker. Whatever it was, here was a man who would not take it anymore.

I saw him standing in the food delivery area next to the bar. Suddenly, as if a cannon had gone off inside his head, he slammed the fish supper onto the floor and stomped on it ferociously, throwing in a few tae kwon do moves to finish it off. He stood back, quivering, and screamed such a ghastly scream that heads peered over the bar to see who had just been murdered. The poor little fish bones lay splattered among the flecks of white meat.

I felt as if my stomach had been kicked out of me. This was worse than having to endure a neighboring asshole nation for three centuries. It took a second for the shock to pass and then I flew at the murderer, like Braveheart flew at the bastard English at the Battle of Stirling.

As I reached him, other Korean forces in the immediate vicinity had crossed the DMZ, the area between bartenders and general public, and were wrestling with the assailant. Before I could attack him with a pot of boiling bar coffee, he broke free and fled.

I picked up the fish supper and folded it back into the newspaper. The chips were mush, and the fish was torn asunder. In somber mood, I placed the carcass in the trash can. I thought about storming down the alley to the chip shop to thrust the murdering bastard's head into the oil but someone asked me, "Is my food ready yet?"

I went home queasy. I switched on *The Chapel*. The things you did to get to sleep! I squeezed a few inches of the tire around my waist.

"It's not a good year," I said to Ben and Jerry.

Steven, the cat, had died. I wondered why it hadn't moved in so long. Sadness hung over the family.

The Dragons were losing players like a cancer victim losing muscle, too. The squad had shrunk from about sixteen to twelve. My kid had abandoned all desire for playing. He was now begging for swimming lessons by practicing his front crawl on the living room floor.

"You have to stick it out to the end," I said.

"But I thought you said it was about sticking it in," he countered.

He was right. I had lost the plot. Sticking it in. Was that the summation of my coaching philosophy, encouraging kids to be rough with other kids, a verifiable recipe for maiming? It was a common thing in any second half of soccer, when you were losing badly, to resort to negative play. The players became distracted, the tiredness set in, the mind wandered, and the pressure of having to come up with an alternative story line to the end of the game was a huge pain, like a kick in the gonads. But what could you do but look at yourself and say, How can I get better? You made some substitutions. That was what you did.

After a few hours of ghastly sleep, I went to the field for game 8 feeling sick, my stomach wracked with cramps, my mood dark. Watching the fish and chips massacre had led me to reflect on the poison I had been feeding the team. "Getting stuck in" was a total failure.

I gathered the squad.

"Today we are getting what?"

"Stuck in," they said lamely.

"No. Not anymore. Instead, I'm going to give you a magical Scottish potion called Bovril. It will make you run fast. Drink!" I said, pulling out my flask.

They ran away.

Il Duce came up.

"Ready?" he said.

"Try some of this," I told him.

"What is it?"

"It'll put a spring in your ass. It's Scottish."

He took a swig, but I guessed he didn't like it much by the way he spewed it halfway across the field.

"Mamma mia. That's not scotch!"

"Scotch? What do you think I am? An alcoholic? We're coaching kids here."

As my guts turned to sludge, I watched game 8 slurry away and join the lake of stinking defeat. I said nothing and I offered no advice to the team. I thought about taking the Bovril flask over to the opponents at halftime and offering their players "a hit" but the stench of resignation rose in my throat and burned me. Trying to be tough, encouraging kids to be hard, was pathetic. Kicking people was wrong.

Dear Reverend Murray,

I was the victim of a culinary crime. Being Scottish, too, I thought that you should hear about this. I have tried Imodium and other stuff but I'm still hogging the bowl. Please pray for my gastrointestinal pipes that they don't burst. I've not been sleeping. I had bad dreams. In my nightmare I saw hundreds of terrorists building a pyramid of Big Macs like the ones they have in Egypt and they climbed to the top and started jumping up and down on it, screaming Allah! Allah! or whatever these terrorists say when they are murdering Americans. All the ketchup flowed into the River Nile and turned it red and all the meat was squashed and horrible.

This kind of vision, Reverend, is proof that we need a robust military to prevent these types of culinary terrorist acts becoming reality. We need right-wing troops because the left wing will do nothing to stop our burgers being abused. I have been working on a project with modeling clay to build a plane that can fly on only one wing, a right wing. Are you interested in investing in my start-up, an engine company, Right Wing Planes, Inc.?

I am still having problems with my soccer team and I hope that I can get over this period and find peace. I heard that Jesus was into peace, but I'm not too sure, so correct me if I'm wrong.

Yours faithfully,
Alan Black

THE SPORTING GREEN

SPECIAL EDITION

Suffer little children. Suffer the man. American youth is in crisis. Our future is at risk. Besides having to deal with the pimping of violence through gadgets, Hollywood, and school shooters, our kids are also facing a crisis in an area of their lives that should be warm and rewarding. Playing youth sports should be the training ground that inspires kids to the promise of leadership, and the dream of taking control on the bridge of enterprise. Sadly, we have to report that this once rich fabric of the nation is being rent asunder by malign forces, inherently un-American.

Just walk to the playing fields of our land on any given Saturday and watch irate adults throwing abuse grenades at children; look at the well-heeled moms and dads standing on the sidelines blaring Junior's name—"Noah!

Noah!"—a constant, hysterical, verbal pitch invasion; witness the squirming body language and turning away in horror when Junior screws up. Kids notice. Kids hear things. Kids remember.

But it's not just the coffee-jazzed parents that are poisoning our youth. The standards of coaching have plummeted like a black day on Wall Street. Ignorant, untrained, angry, and in some cases foreign-born, these instructors have allowed the practice of coaching to degenerate into a mire of failure and recrimination. This newspaper calls on the government to hold hearings into the state of youth coaching in our country.

We have some practical suggestions that would go a long way to correcting this deviated septum of the national spirit. Our goalless local team, the Dragons, is a gross anomaly on many levels, but their plight does highlight many of the problems. Leagues should have the power to fire failed coaches. Coaching should not be about the incision of negative thoughts into a child's mind.

Second, we have limited background checks for gun purchases, and that makes sense, but what about background checks for coaches? Are bad coaches not holding a gun to the head of our kids? A new breed of moral hounds should sniff out those who illustrate contempt for the American way of life, by abandoning responsibility and demoting the American values of morality and fun. Impartial parental oversight committees should have the power to recommend investigations into bad coaching. Just as aliens have to take a test to become citizens of the republic, they should be required to take a test before coaching our sons and daughters. Undesirable foreigners, like the current coach of the Dragons, can bring the calcified prejudice of negativity and low achievement of their native lands to our suburban avenues. A simple questionnaire would help eliminate the unwanted from youth coaching. We suggest the following as a blueprint:

If your team loses, do you:

1. Blame the team
2. Blame yourself
3. Blame America

If a parent complains to you about your decisions, do you:

1. Smile
2. Think, "What do they know?"
3. Blame the team

Coaching should be about:

1. Winning
2. Losing
3. Fun

American values are best illustrated by:

1. Ronald Reagan
2. Ted Kennedy's drink bill
3. The actions of Siegfried and Roy's tiger

CHAPTER 20

Help

One night, at about this time, I woke up in agony. My gut felt like a swollen soccer ball. Doubled in two, then doubled in three, I prayed for an explosion. I lay on the sofa and watched C-Span, hoping it would numb me, but the live coverage of a debate from the House of Representatives only made me feel worse and finally sent me to the emergency room.

At the hospital, after a long, challenging waiting game among the walk-in wounded, I finally got admitted and a young man shaved my chest, attached wires, and said that I reminded him of Sean Connery. A man in the bed next to me, behind a curtain, was breathing heavily and whimpering. As for me, no heart attack, and nothing on the X-ray. The doctor came in. Life slowed. What would he pronounce?

Life, or death.

"You need to make a big fart and you need to make some lifestyle changes, Mr. Black. How much stress do you have in your life?"

"None."

I'm sure they could see the word "liar" on the shadows of the X-ray.

"Any trouble sleeping?"

"No. I use religion to get to sleep."

"Any nightmares?"

"I woke up sweating, thinking I had been arrested for killing my lawn."

"How is your stool?"

"It's Bovril."

"Have you tried relaxation techniques? Like yoga?"

"No, but I will, Doctor. I unflinchingly obey medical advice."

Bought a block, bought a mat, went around saying *Om*. Yoga was another fiber in the healthy colon of the liberal community in which I found myself. Being a member of the YMCA was popular round my way. I would see soccer moms head to the Y with their yoga mats under their arms. I popped my head into the gym and saw old men pumping iron. I saw shapely ladies rotating to jazzercise. Seniors pawed like cats in tai chi. I should get to know these people, get involved. The current mayor was probably in here every day sweating to the oldies and shaking hands with voters. Joining the Y would expand my visibility and help my exploratory committee for my future mayoral campaign.

Maybe the yoga would open the doors to a fresh start for the Dragons and myself, too. God knows they needed enlightenment. I just had to find the transforming platform that would project a winning, healthy energy into the games. Losing was a state of mind. It could be overcome. So I signed up for the yoga classes. There, a newbie Scotsman who looked like a drowned dog performed a transforming triangle pose for the first time.

The YMCA gymnasium had a wall of mirrors designed to help the practitioner line up the outstretched limbs while allowing furtive spying on the others in their poses. The mirrors told no lie. My down dog pose betrayed a curvature of the spine that would have pleased a Muslim looking for a crescent. I couldn't cross my legs or touch my toes. My skeleton creaked under the blanket. The teacher was preaching,

Take a breath.

The muscles screamed as they filled with oxygen.

Breathe.

The head swam with blood.

Hold it!

Directly behind me on the floor was a face with a soft beard that fitted the profile of a man whose roommates were likely blow-up dolls. The energy from his secret yogic eye trick fed straight into my sense of being watched from behind. You always knew when someone was staring at your ass. It was part of the survival instinct.

Suspiciously supple for a man, he obviously enjoyed a deep widening of the groin. Long, thrusting breaths crept from the well in his lungs. I made the mistake of turning round.

He smiled at me.

I froze in Arctic pose.

He spoke to me.

I stood in deaf pose.

He seemed perplexed.

I offered dumb pose.

He turned away.

Thank God pose.

And then the teacher said, "Partner up."

Partner up. What the fuck was that?

I looked for a girl.

No chance. They fled to each other.

The man with the soft beard came up with a yoga belt in his hand.

"Hello, partner," he said.

He straddled me from behind, holding a strap around my waist, raising my butt up high as I stretched for a deeper down dog.

"Does that feel good?" he said.

My stomach did jumping jacks as my butt muscles barricaded the door.

I rolled up the mat, went home, and used my block for chopping meat for lunch.

• • • •

I tried meditation. I found my space. I closed my eyes and saw the street people around my workplace being loaded into a large washing machine. I envisioned the massacred fish supper reborn as a blue dolphin splashing through the waves. I saw the Dragons' breath burn like a match. I saw the team running from a juggernaut down the highway. I saw images from space with backyard laundry lines all over America, hanging out clothes. My nostrils filled with the scents of many kitchens. Breezes wafted in, flavors of the month. Great piles of discarded gadgets sparked and flashed, the planet buzzed, hot, electric, and primed to explode. Great worms slinked across the plains, and the fires had burned down the little house on the prairie. Laura Ingles was dead. The Waltons had been evicted. It was Good Night, Jim-Bob.

I read in my Zen guidebook that the goal of the higher states of meditation was to abandon hope. Hope ruined lives. A faster route to this hopeless state of bliss, instead of sitting cross-legged staring at the back of your eyelids for twenty years, was to coach the fucking Dragons. They could kill hope in a single half of soccer.

But hope was the ultimate drug. I was as addicted to it as the next sucker. And being a Scottish soccer fanatic, it was a very serious debilitating condition. Like any drug you needed a steps program to get off it. I invented one, the cure for the hope dope.

A STEPS PROGRAM TO GET OFF HOPE

STEP ONE:
I must accept my powerlessness over crappy young soccer players who are making my life as a coach unmanageable.

STEP TWO:

I must accept that the Dragons scoring a goal is out of my hands. Only a higher power could deliver results.

STEP THREE:

I must turn the destiny of the team over to God, as I understand him.

Some nights he was speaking in an Arkansas tongue reading from a toughened hide Bible, sitting in a leather chair, blasting the ignoramuses for their lack of understanding and poor handwriting in the searching letters, while cursing a nation of sinners and abortionists riddled with liberal judges and homosexuals keen to strip the sword from the Lord's pale hand. As I understood him, he wasn't likely to be home, just as he wasn't home during the Holocaust or the Highland Clearances or when the Dragons needed a goal.

STEP FOUR:

Take a moral inventory.

Man takes position as a coach in a soccer team. Brings childhood experience and appreciation of soccer to the position. Imagines that giving back to the community will help him get elected mayor and rekindle his childhood love of soccer. Sets out with enthusiastic targets only to be blown off course by the worst soccer team in the history of the game. Loathes them for it. Fails to build links to other immigrant parents in the team. Resents Iranians in cotton Dockers and Italians dressed as Kurds. Finds offense in defense. And vice versa.

STEP FIVE:

Am I ready to have God, as I understand him, remove the defects of my character?

You betcha! I was on the gurney; God was washing his hands in the antechamber next to the surgery. Surrounded by angels dressed in naughty nurses' uniforms, he said with a deep voice, "Let's fix this man."

The anesthetist pumped high-octane marijuana into my nose and mouth. "Count backward from ten, nine, eigh . . ."

"Scalpel." The rip went from head to toe.

"We'll start with the Scottish blockage first. Yes, I can see deep-fried haggis and deep-fried pizza stuck in the lower bowel and there are the nodes of irrepressible hope and desire. They seem to have spread throughout the system. I haven't seen one of these since before there was light—a supersuggestive ego condition with a massive arsenal of blamethrowers. This man has a finger-pointing complex of the highest degree. Remove it and replace it with a metal plate of humility and acceptance. It's too bad for him at the airport. Just one more piece of surgery and we're done here. Bring in the American smile and stitch it to his face. Patch him up. And Nurse, see me in the antechamber in a few moments to help me get undressed. And don't forget to bill him."

STEP SIX:

I humbly ask God, as I understand him, to remove my shortcomings.

Il Duce had to go.

STEP SEVEN:

Make a list of all the people I have harmed as a result of being addicted to hope.

I had injected the Dragons with hope at the start of the season, by filling up their emotional tanks with rousing cascades of expectation. I would have to include the parents on my sorry list. I had encouraged them to believe that soccer was a fulfilling pastime for their kids and that I had the right mettle for the job. And I had made kids cry. What kind of coach makes a kid cry? I had harmed coaching. I had harmed America's future in my own small way. I would write a letter to the president and apologize. Someone once yelled at me, "Go back to Cuba or wherever you're fucking from." Maybe they were right.

STEP EIGHT:

Directly make amends to those you have hurt.

How could I take step eight? It was bad enough drawing up a list of the harmed for my mea culpa but to have to apologize to them in person would take a steel will wrought in the burning mill of failure. Individual apologies to players may spark an inquiry by parents alarmed about the exact meaning of the words "sorry for harming you," so a more, safe collective expression of remorse would suffice. I would gather the team and the parents together and say,

"Listen, kids and parents. I thought we had prospects when we started this season. I believed that we were a team and that we might have a chance of getting a single win, certainly a tie, but what we got instead was high-altitude defeats that required oxygen. So I am deeply sorry that I led you up the mountain of hope. I should have acknowledged at the beginning that you guys totally suck. Please accept my confession. I'll never hurt you with horrible hope again."

• • • •

That was enough of the steps. I was exhausted. It was no wonder alcoholics who had been sober for twenty years looked like shite. Scaling the top twelve steps in the emotional Himalayas, without a flask, was one tall order.

• • • •

At the training field, the warm breeze ran its fingers through the leaves, loosening the straps of the season. The Dragons were set to receive my newly found yogic knowledge, a new coaching philosophy.

"Who knows what yoga is?" I asked.

"Something you eat at breakfast," said Manny.

"Very funny."

"What is it then?"

"It's an Indian practice that helps you stretch out."

We tried down dog with much barking and larking. Warrior one and warrior two were improved upon by throwing in a few kung fu kicks and Hong Kong–phooey chops. The boys twisted and threw their arms up to a T and attempted headstands that toppled like gravestones blown over by laughter.

"Let's try corpse pose," I said. "Lie down flat on your back and pretend that you are dead."

And there they lay, flat out, silent, a dead team of young boys, wiped out, snuffed, waiting for the undertaker.

"Okay. Wake up."

No breeze stirred the trees.

CHAPTER 21

Fair and Balanced

At the next game, I said, "Okay, boys. Listen up. Forget all that stuff about getting stuck in. We're not going to do that nonsense anymore. Just go out and have your fun. That's what your parents want. There's no need for anyone to feel any pressure anymore; it's just a game, so it doesn't matter what the score is, no matter how many goals they score, we're here to play, to make up the numbers, to let it happen as the gods of soccer feel fit. Play anywhere you want. Off you go, now. Have a good game."

A voice behind me said, "Excuse me."

I jumped and turned. There was a league official standing at my ear. Had he heard the abandoned hope strategy? I fought the urge for a deep knee bend. The teeth gritted, a mild ache flashed on a molar. A sinister black garment was in his hand.

"The referee has failed to show up. You'll have to do it."

Countless arrows with poisoned tips had been pulled from my soccer quiver over the years and slung at many match officials. Referees bore the brunt of the soccer fan storms. Every adjective of derision, every verbal nuance of projectile vomit had been dumped on them. To be a referee you needed a sadomasochistic streak. He was the odd man out, the wicked daddy who sent the boy for an early bath or stopped the fun by blowing his pea. And his silly-ass friends ran the line with flags waving at the wrong moment. As a kid at Shawfield, I had cheered as men set fire to the referee's car in the car park.

"You want me to be the ref?" I said incredulously.

"Yes. You are the ref."

I looked at my right-hand man, my Il Duce. His look traveled up from the lower reaches of the atmosphere.

"Today, I run the team," he said.

"Everything will be on time," I replied, "like the trains."

I looked at my old watch. The seconds hand was broken. It stuttered, and was stuck bounding off the same second. I pulled on the referee's black shirt. Immediately, I felt like a fascist.

"Maybe you should wear this," I said to Il Duce. He ignored me.

I walked over to the opposing team coach and extended my hand in a gesture meant to convince him of my impeccable belief in the fair and balanced principles of refereeing. He was Mexican. And his team was made from the proud sons of Mexico.

"You better be fair, amigo," the Mexican said.

"Perfectly fair, señor," I said. "Would you like to call the coin toss or shall I have your team captain decide?"

"We kick off. Fuck the coin toss," he replied.

"No. We must toss the coin."

"Heads!"

"Tails. You lost."

I turned my back and walked across the field. The theme music from *The Good, the Bad, and the Ugly* rattled inside my head. I lengthened my yoga spine and slung my legs forward like Eastwood sliding across the desert. I waited for the gunfire to cut me down, the blood to spill from the heart of the man in black, as the assailants galloped away, their big sombreros flying in the wind.

"Okay, Dragons. Listen up. I'm the referee today and I'm on your side."

I stood in the center circle and gazed around. The birds were twittering in the treetops. I glanced over at the Mexican patrons. I nodded to Il Duce. The teams were waiting for the whistle. I checked the official game watch on my wrist, and gave a signal to the linesmen that the game was about to kick off. Right then, an odd sensation fluttered inside my heart, almost like a dream or a New Age astral projection, and there on the screen I saw myself standing on the field, as seen from above, from the space shuttle perhaps, with thousands of soccer fanatics wrapped into the sweaty blanket of a stadium, waiting for the moment when the breath of the man in black set forward events that would leave imprints on the memories of millions. I looked up at the sky and saw a pigeon soar and hoped that its ass had not just opened. The pea rattled. The Dragons kicked off. The Mexicans could go fuck themselves.

Running with the play, I could instruct the Dragons up close, and things were going better than usual with five minutes played. Manny had cleared a couple of early chances by the Sons of Mexico and our center forward had almost touched the ball.

"Push up," I told the potted fern in need of an evolutionary leap. "Make them play deep."

Over on the sidelines, I could see the Mexican coaches talking to each other, making hand gestures that looked like fists crushing into palms. Suddenly, a Son of Mexico started a mazy run through the midfield. Instinctively, I knew trouble was coming. I picked up my legs and flew down the field. A sneaky direct cut in front of the threat, distracting him for a second, was enough to allow Manny to step in and boot the ball clear. No one seemed to have noticed on *el otro lado*. We could get a tie here, I thought, if I can keep myself in the game.

Seconds later, a wily Son of Mexico pulled back his boot and let fly a bullet. I tried to get out of the way of the ball but it ricocheted off my leg and went out behind the goal.

The Mexican linesman was pointing to the corner spot.

"Goal kick," I yelled, pointing at the six-yard box.

The first howls of protest arose from the Mexican sidelines.

The Latin lads now ate into the game with a diet of affront. And soon they had the ball in the back of the Dragons' net. The Mexican linesman started off toward the centerline, passing the cheers from the Mexican families happy to see the first goal of what they knew would be many. But as they

were celebrating the goal, the MacGringo referee was pointing to the penalty box, yelling:

"Offside!"

The Mexicans took the inevitable second between joy and
interruption badly. They rounded on me as if I was meat
being chopped for a *carne asada* burrito.

"It's offside," I told them. "He was a mile offside."

I went to the linesman and admonished him.

"You have to pay attention to the offside rule, señor. These
kids will never learn the game if you are unwilling to uphold
the laws of the game. If it happens again, the match will be
abandoned and recorded as a tie and you will be reported to
the league as a cheat."

There was now a clear and present danger that my balls
would be thrust on a skewer and barbecued on a grill in
Baja.

So what! I remembered the Alamo. Davy Crockett was
Scottish, goddamnit! And today the Dragons would be given
a decent chance to get a tie. By Christ in his soccer cleats, we
deserved it, for our suffering had been long enough. Humiliated, trounced, annihilated, exterminated, obliterated, that
was our season, and we had given up hope of a win. But
now we were willing to tie at any cost, and if cheating the
Mexicans was the means to the end, I would suggest that
the Mexicans take a good look at their own history of soccer
cheating. They fucking invented the diving soccer player!

Manny clattered into a Son of Mexico like a Humvee
squashing an Iraqi peasant. The Mexican coaches barked for

the whistle indicating a foul. I would give them what they were looking for. I blew.

"Okay, kid. Get up. That was a dive. I'm going to have to give you a yellow card."

"It was a dive," I yelled at the Mexican bench. "If you don't want him to get sent off, send him to swimming lessons because that is where he belongs."

They were beside themselves with rage. The Mexican linesman was waving his flag furiously.

"What's that?" I said. "Some kind of Mexican semaphore? An SOS call because they can't handle being on the short end of the stick for once? Fuck them!"

The seconds ticked down to the halftime whistle. I saw our halftime snack of bananas waiting to be skinned and devoured. For once, at halftime, the Dragons would not be skidding on the tossed-away peels of slaughter.

I blew the whistle for the end of the half and the Mexicans went mad. We had made it to halftime without conceding a goal. Our halftime talk would have meaning today. But there would be no return to hope. The Mexicans had stripped me of the whistle, demanding the black top of the referee; one of their number would put it on for the second half, when revenge against MacGringo would be happily delivered.

"Ye're welcome tay it, ya fascist," I said in a bagpipe tone.

I walked over to the Mexican linesman and said, "Hand over the flag. It's our turn."

He dropped it on the ground.

"Keep the fucking flag down in the second half, no matter

if we're offside by miles," I told Il Duce, the new linesman. He looked impressive with that flag, like he could have been on a railway platform waving to the train driver to get the train moving out of the station. He knew the score when it came to cheating, but the inevitable unfolded quickly and soon buckets of goals were served up by the Sons of Mexico.

But as our goal was being nailed up again, a shock of golden hair, like a fleece that had blown over the horizon with the bright fingers of dawn, caught my eye. And beneath those curls was a kid wearing a Dragons top. He was urging the team on in the face of the onslaught. He picked up the ball in the midfield and held on to it, like he had a right to it. It took three Mexicans to rob him. He threw up his body like a barrier, a massive wall of denial, sweat lashing from his forehead, as if sickened by the gross assaults on our team. He ministered, willing the weakened Dragons around him to believe in the possibility.

He was yelling, "Follow me. Look up. Go forward. To their goal."

Who was this kid?

He was the one who didn't celebrate Christmas.

THE SPORTING GREEN

A DISGRACE TO THE RULEBOOK

Around the time Germans were inventing the first coughing prototype of the automobile, and Queen Victoria still sat on the potty in England with the globe in her lily-white hand, a manufacturer called Hudson of the Acme Whistle Company invented a little device that would change world history.

For too long, villains in London had managed to evade the long arm of the law by being able to outrun Constable Corner of the Yard. The puffing copper could now call for assistance from his uniformed fellows by blowing in his new shrill whistle. Soon, another type of policeman would be using the blustery little blower to call foul—the soccer referee.

Before the invention of the whistle, a referee was constrained to waving his starched handkerchief to get the attention of players who had just hacked the legs off an opponent. Now with his whistle in hand, he could stop the action dead in its tracks. With their peas, if not their q's, referees finally got respect.

With the evolution of the referee's authority came the evolution of the referee's uniform. The black shirt, a potent symbol of twentieth-century fascism, replaced the original blazer. With the arrival of the cards, yellow and red, a referee could give banishment with a straight-arm salute. Refereeing satisfies fascist tendencies in some men, as surgeons satisfy their psychopathic needs to slit open the living with sharp knives.

On Saturday past, a more ugly display of refereeing would have been hard to find, a biased perversion introduced by the Dragons' head coach. With the match referee likely stuck like a thrombosis in the legs of a traffic jam, the league official handed the black shirt and the whistle to the Scottish coach, obviously ignorant to the fact that the desperate and humiliated would take advantage of any opportunity.

Yellow-carding a victim of a foul for diving was not the worst of the egregious bias. A fairly executed goal was chopped off for offside when the attacker was at least five yards onside. Haranguing the Mexican team coach with insult and borderline xenophobic contempt, Coach Black's reputation was sent to a new low.

The coach having been stripped of the black shirt at halftime, the game returned to a normal state of affairs, with the Dragons losing handily. There was a spark of light in the blackness, however—the encouraging play of a previously unnoticed Dragons midfielder. Not much is known of the kid with the blond curls except that he may have hailed from somewhere in the East. His strength in holding off opponents with graceful sleights of foot, and his strange appearance of seemingly gliding over the grass as if he were walking on water, added to his allure.

At the postmatch press conference, Black assailed the press in his usual blustering manner. "I'm sick and tired of coming down here after games to listen to you harp on about how bad things are. Here's some news for you to print: We don't care anymore. We don't need to hear the sounds of your tinny little pens scratching away, cliché after cliché, when not one of you bastards has ever kicked a ball in your lives. **** you!"

As the *Sporting Green* is part of a corporate network of publications that supports the family values of our shareholders, we sadly cannot help you fill in the stars. But know this: the Dragons can soon move from the sporting pages to the obituary column.

CHAPTER 22

All Change

The full moon was so bright burglars stayed at home. I was outside looking at my lawn.

"Why won't it grow?" I asked Ben and Jerry.

They shrugged.

"I'm giving up this Cherry Garcia flavor for good. What am I thinking, eating the ice cream corpse of a fat guy who died in a rehab clinic, a guy who has an asteroid named after him? This is ungrateful dead flavor."

I looked at the moon. "Shine some light on the matter, will you? Your pal the sun has done fuck all but kill the lawn. How about some moonbeams to get the grass to grow?"

I turned on the new hose and propped it up against the stars.

"I'll turn it off before I go to bed. I need to write a letter."

Dear Reverend Murray,

> *This is my last letter to you. You will never hear from me again. I have lost faith. I am going to bed. I can't wait*

*around anymore hoping to see Jesus appear in the sky, I
can't hope anymore that you will read my letters out on
the air, I can't hope anymore that my lawn will grow, I
can't hope anymore that the Dragons will score a goal.
I've given up hope and I feel better already. Now things
can happen. And here's a lesson for you, Reverend. The
more you say Jesus is coming, the more he won't. Once
you say, "Don't bother, Jesus, we know you're too busy,"
he'll show up unannounced looking for his dinner, like
he did in the Bible. I understand that you want to keep
hope alive. You need the flock's tidings to keep you in
wing buckets from KFC. But, Reverend, one day, even
you will give up hope.*

> *Yours unfaithfully,*
> *Alan Black*

Years ago, on Sunday mornings at nine a.m. on Scottish
telly, a program teaching lip reading caught my attention
and turned me into a regular viewer. While the nation slept
off the hangovers of the Saturday night, I would be wide
awake mastering the art of listening without hearing.

Lip reading had helped me pick up conversations between girls as they discussed what a great-looking guy I
was. Bingo! Troublemakers and thugs in pubs had sent me
lip messages prompting my escape through the back door
before a hand could hit my face. Ouch! How many people
have said once in their lives, I wish I knew what they were
saying about me?

And now I could see the parents chatting to each other

on the sidelines. I picked up a "no good . . . useless . . . Scotland," all in the same sentence. But now it did not matter. My record was abysmal. We had lost to the blind, been mauled by the dwarves, one of whom was deaf, and had been slaughtered by the Mexicans. Who would beat us next? The quadriplegics?

"I've abandoned all hope for the Dragons," I told Il Duce. "Let's try your suggestion about mixing up the team. Offense as defense and vice versa."

For sure, my early season anxieties about fitting in with the suburbanites were receding. I was less self-conscious. The teeth-whitening strips were working, the haircut a little longer but mundane, and my persistence in wearing the Dockers had forced me into the pattern, but I had failed to make any connections, never mind friends. The casual nature of my reticence had hampered my popularity. My conversation was weighed down by tiredness from bartending, a job that sent your social skills into cynical retreat (contrary to the perception that bartending was a happy-go-lucky type of lifestyle). I should take classes in conversational skills. Maybe I should change my accent and sound like an American.

I was taken back to the day I became a citizen of the republic, the day I secured my vote, the moment I could stand shoulder to shoulder with happiness and the Constitution, to be part of the right that allowed you to buy a gun at Wal-Mart like a good patriot. "Give me liberty or give me death" was my favorite American phrase.

I stood with others reciting the Pledge of Allegiance before a judge. A guy in front of me was crossing his fingers behind his back. After the ceremony, a gorgeous Asian lady with a sunshine smile crossed my path outside the auditorium.

"Where are you from?" she asked in a voice of melted caramels.

"I'm from Scotland."

"You have a very thick accent," she said.

She handed me her business card.

ACCENT ELIMINATION
Take care of your old accent now!
Get a new American accent!
The Key to Financial Success in America.

In later years, I thought about her. When I called the cable company to complain about the snow on my screen they kept asking, "What, what, what?" When I said "thirteen," Americans were convinced it was "thirty." I worked in a shop before bar life and asked a fellow male employee if he was staying late, "to half six?" He thought I was gay.

Should I ditch the Scottish brogue? Give up the ghost? Drown my voice with dudes, likes, reallys, awesomes, cools? I rented John Wayne movies. I would give it a go. I would practice on the team.

I rolled into the next practice and announced, "Doods—
get off your horse and drink your milk!"

"What?" said Manny.

"'Scuse me there, Manny, my homey dood."

A roar of laughter came from the Dragons' lair.

"Why you doods laughin' at me?"

"You sound stoopid."

I could see my son wince in embarrassment.

Fortunately, at that moment Il Duce arrived.

"Okay. Let's move the players around today. New positions," he said.

"I'm all for a new language for the team, dood. I think all
that jive about being tough 'n' leavin' stains on defenders
was a big yahoo!"

He looked down at his immaculate Dockers.

"What you know about da Roman history?" I asked.

"Not much," he said.

"I like *I, Claudius*. Did you see that awesome show on the
boob toob?"

"There was a show about Claudius on the what?"

"The television."

"No. I don't know it."

"Well. Claudius was the emperor, the main man, buddy
guy, picked by . . ."

"The guards," he said.

I looked at the parents.

"Hey, remember you said you had never heard of Scotland, when I thought you were a Kurd?" I said.

"No," he replied.

"Forget it. Have you ever thought about changing your accent?" I said to him.

• • • •

And Saturday came again. I stepped back. It was time to work my magic. So I mingled with the parents and started up conversations, softening my r's, strumming my twang, and avoiding the unbearable conversation that their children were fucking useless at soccer. I minced through the weather, hailed the mockery of the commander in chief, lamented the state of the freeways, and suggested that having an Austrian in charge of California might be a little like the Dead Kennedys song "California Über Alles" coming true. I chatted to Dr. John, the shrink. I let it be known, loud and clear, that I was a happy man, a family guy, a real pleasant dood, my kid was in the team, I volunteered for the position, I had taken over the team, I was seeking long-term smile solutions and repairs to my dietary bridge, no more Bovril! I shopped at the mall, I was working on my lawn, planning a run for office, and I was a convert to yoga.

"What an awesome day for soccer," I said.

"Run for office?"

"Mayor."

Dr. John laughed.

"You sound different," he said, his mind presumably flicking through the pages of his psychiatric manual looking for the delusions of grandeur diagnosis. At which point, Il Duce joined us.

"Take over the reins of the chariot," I said.

It was his day in the hot seat. He got to move the players around to different positions. And soon the ball was in the enemy half. And then it was there again. And then again. And attached to it was the kid with the blond curls. Who was that guy? He made a run for their goal. I had nearly forgotten all about that four-letter word. He moved into the eighteen-yard box and fired a drive. I went woozy as if I had been plunged into a barrel of Jack Daniel's. The ball screeched past the post by inches.

It was our first shot of the season.

Then moments later, the golden boy burst through again, against the odds, and he slipped two tackles and headed to the edge of the eighteen-yard box. He stopped briefly, looked around, saw no support, and fired a strike that struck the inside of the post. The goalie was beaten. The ball trundled along the line, baubles of earth poking away from the goal, others pointing inward to the net, the ball popping over every one of them as if it were in a roulette wheel bouncing around waiting to drop joy or frustration into the gambler's lap. I sent supersonic om waves to the bouncing ball.

Ommmmmmmmmm.

I used every mental power I had to will that ball over that line. I blew little whiffs of air. I jumped up and down hoping to shake the field. But God was against me. I should never have sent that letter of resignation to the reverend in Arkansas.

After the game was over (with a better loss than usual) and the players gone, I was there alone with my son. I put him in the car and told him I'd be right back. I walked to the goal where our first goal of the season was nearly scored. With a ball in my hand, one small step at a time, I paced the length of the goal line. It was hard to stay on the straight and narrow. The ball had moved along here and hit the other post and spun away from being caught in the net, like the single fish that escapes the catch. I looked at the post. There was a mark on it where the ball had made contact. I spat on my sleeve and wiped it off.

I turned, and saw my kid watching me through the car window. I looked down one last time at the ball.

"Alas, poor Yorrick! I knew him well."

I pulled back my instep, and hammered it home.

"You fucking bastard," I yelled, at everything and nothing.

THE SPORTING GREEN

THE CURLS ON THE BALL

In a stunning development, the Dragons took a shot at goal on Saturday and hit the woodwork. The kid with the blond curls picked the ball up in his own half and made his way forward, expanding his territory with a fast-paced acceleration that left the assembled defenders rootless and dispossessed. This mystery player has emerged from the wilderness, and has inspired a team. He has shown the Dragons a most unlikely possibility—the goal. Defying the record, he settled the ball in the opponents' half for long periods of time, bringing Dragons players with him. Some of the Dragons players had never been in an opponent's half throughout the entire season.

His rifled shot that spun off the post and tantalizingly trundled across the gaping goal brought life back to the corpse. Several Dragons made successful passes for the first time this season. Manny headed the ball clear and the Dragons' goalie, Dolt, as he is affectionately nicknamed by the fans, made several decent saves.

But no single player can carry the burden of a team of losers for a whole game. The Dragons finally lost by a sizable margin but they suffered their lowest defeat of the year.

At the postmatch press conference, a relaxed and smiling Coach Black suggested that hope was a fixture that could never be extinguished.

"We nearly scored a goal. We are back. And you can look at our lowest defeat of the year as the opening salvo in a new campaign for the final few games of the season. Victory is our target. I suggest that you members of the press, who have been nothing but savage and venereal in your itchiness to condemn the Dragons this season, fill your wells with more ink and open your dictionaries for positive adjectives because we are turning the season around. And here is a four-letter word for you to ponder, although it might be a bit difficult for some of you journalists to spell. Hope. You better believe it. It's our new bipolar philosophy."

CHAPTER 23

No Substitute

week later, I still had my head down as I left the house for work. I had flooded the street by forgetting to turn off the hose on the night I wrote my fateful final letter to Arkansas. It had taken a while for Noah's calamity to subside. A stranger had knocked furiously on my door, my wife had yelled at me, and I had staggered from bed and waded into the lake and turned off the serpent's head. I was up to my neck in shame. Cars glided through the water like Loch Ness monsters. The patriot across the street was dismissive. Styrofoam cups and Taco Bell flotsam had drifted down the street creek. A police car stopped by. Every living creepy-crawly, spider, and worm had drowned. The silver lining was in the dead weeds that floated on the surface of my man-made lake. Later that day, once the water had receded, I pulled on the golf shoes and went for another round of holes on my soaking lawn. I grabbed the seed bag and laid them out on the soil. I spread fertilizer on top. I would wait and hope again.

It was slow at work, a few beers here and there, long periods of standing still staring at the drips from the broken beer tap. I thought about the Dragons. Was I fucking nuts telling myself that I was giving up on hoping? I was the head coach. These parents had paid a chunk of money to have the team coached. How many times had I said that? Repetition was the stamp of coaching, and bad writing. But who cared? Goddamnit, we had nearly scored! It was so close. I had tasted it and it tasted good. I wanted more! I wanted a goal! I was off the hope wagon with a bang!

I grabbed a rocks glass and downed a shot of Jameson. This was soccer! As if dry existential meditative philosophy would be enough to keep me happy. What tosh! Had not Albert Camus been a goalkeeper? Had he not said, "Everything I learned about morality and obligations, I owe to soccer"? The kid with the blond curls had almost scored a goal! I slammed another Jameson. Imagine his shot had gone in. Give us another one! What would it have done for the Dragons? Revolution! Throw off the old order of defeat. We can score more. We can win! Strip the winds of fortune. The Dragons needed more hope. We needed the high-powered stuff, the skunk, the grade A, the Colombian that was on sale in the streets around the bar.

Now I was drunk. I thought back to the World Cup Finals in 1974 when Brazil played Holland. I had prayed to God in the toilet at halftime, to give Brazil hope for the second half, and within minutes of the second half starting Brazil nearly scored, although in the end God was Dutch. When Olivia

Newton-John in her pretty little cardigan sang "Hopelessly Devoted to You" in *Grease* she was singing to me, not Mr. Scientology Travolta. I was a Bob Hope fan and he lived in Palm Springs where the lawns were super green. I sent money to Bill Clinton's campaign in 1992 and he came from a town called Hope in Arkansas, down the road from the Murrays. Clinton gave me hope that one day I could be mayor of my American hamlet. My favorite Roman quote was *dum spiro, spero* by Cicero.

There was always tomorrow to get things done. Hope and procrastination slept together. There could be a next season for the Dragons. Who knew? Maybe the team would stick together. Maybe the kid with the blond curls had a brother, or a squad of soccer-playing disciples, cut from his cloth. The Dragons may not retire from soccer at such a young age and hate Scottish people for the rest of their lives. My coaching career may not be over. The big hope dope. I had another Jameson.

· · · ·

Around then, my tooth began to hurt. And then it hurt more. And soon there was a mining operation on my gum. The cursed, venomous stang was sounding off inside my mouth like clashing trash can lids in *Stomp*. Flashing lights blinded my eyes as I poured a compound mixture of aspirin and whiskey onto the riot of pain. The mouth swelled like a bubo, hot, burning, shedding ache like a mangy dog losing its fur. I was stripped to the waist. Sweat broke open on my scalp. I tried all the positions known to mankind: horizontal, vertical, wrapped around the table, fetal, catatonic, stretched, and finally inverted, which only stopped when my neck cracked. I scratched my face like a desperate rat trying to escape a trap. More whiskey, more aspirin; the froth inside the mouth was fomenting and bubbling. I looked in the mirror, mouth broken, and finally my eyes rolled back. Dr. Jekyll changed into Mr. Hyde.

Every fucking book on the shelf was thrown down, torn apart, chewed pages ripped from the classics and stuffed into the rotting molar—Hemingway's *For Whom the Bell Tolls,* that fat alcoholic slob, and James Joyce's *Ulysses,* that Irish pervert—finally pages from their books being put to good use as a packing ram for the rotted hole in my blackening tooth. I kicked the telly. I booted a ball against the wall and it flew back at me in self-defense. A fork was stabbed into the kitchen cabinet and finally I arrived at the place where it is always darkest, just before it goes totally black.

People died from toothache.

On awakening, a baseball had formed inside my mouth like some preemptive attack on my future campaign for decent soccer fields. A friend recommended a Hungarian dentist who operated on immigrants for cheap. It sounded dodgy but it was either Transylvanian surgery or death.

I drove to her office like a madman, the sweat lashing off me. I raced to the big seat, the interrogation light swung over my fat jaw, the glasses of the dentist reflected the gape, as the instruments were inserted and the autopsy commenced on the molar.

"It's dead. We'll have to cut it out," said the Hungarian dentist, "but before we can, we must get the swelling down. Take this to a pharmacist. You need painkillers, too."

Now I had dope to go with the hope and the Jameson.

CHAPTER 24

Green

The last St. Paddy's Day in the bar. The beer was green. Corned beef and cabbage soured the air. The Guinness was sitting patiently waiting for Ireland to be united. The band was stomping out the Rebel songs. Adding insult to injury were morons asking for Irish car bombs and black and tans. Our bar was mobbed with one-day Paddies.

A young American woman asked, "What part of Ireland are you from?"

"The Scottish part," I said.

"That's so cool," she said.

She didn't know the difference. Scotland. Ireland. It wasn't England! And they didn't care. All they wanted was to get drunk on the best excuse of the year and be served Guinness by a guy with a brogue.

* * * *

I thought of Ireland as I saw the luck of the Emerald Isle appear on my lawn. Little pops of green were shooting through the soil, small leprechauns of mischievous grass happily bathing in the morning dew. I got down on my knees and stroked them. The waves of the golden sun lapped on my yard. I put my ear to the sod. I could hear my grass growing.

"Thank you, St. Patrick. You've driven the snakes from my soil."

I looked across the street at the neighbor's house.

"It's born again!" I yelled.

I couldn't wait for the Fourth of July to come around. By then I would have a thick forest of lawn. And on it, I would invite my friends over for a barbecue party. Old Glory would be flying high above the triumph of the resurrection. I would play the Mormon Tabernacle Choir on my boom box.

But I would have to be careful in tending this sod back to fullness. I did not want to flood the plains again. I needed to keep the weed cancer away, too. I went to the Home Depot to find a grass expert.

"Hey, I've just saved my lawn, Operation Lawn Rescue. Man, you should have seen it. It looked like . . . you don't want to know. Listen, I want to keep it on the recovery path. I'm Scottish and this is my first American lawn and I want people to notice it. What can I do to keep it moving in the right direction? Is there such a thing as lawn steroids?"

"Keep the soil aerated—did I already mention that to you?—and water lightly three times a week, early in the morning before the sun gets too high. And you'll soon be needing this, my friend."

He reached behind him and pulled out a Scotts reel lawn mower.

"Twenty-inch cutting width; height range one to three inches; quick-snap height adjusters; dual wheel tracking; five-spider, five-blade ball bearing reel; ten-inch composite wheels with radial tread tires; six-inch rear tracking wheels; heat-treated blades; welded reel hood; loop-style handle with foam grip; two-year warranty. Made in the USA."

"Amazing," I said. "My first lawn mower."

"And it's made by Scotts. That's close to Irish, right?"

Back home, I unloaded my purchase out of my trunk. I hoped the neighbor could see this suburban moment. I was the proud owner of a lawn mower and I would soon mow my own lawn. I needed no help to keep my homestead thriving. Things were on the upswing.

Now that I had grass again, I pulled out a new ice cream flavor.

"Hey, Ben and Jerry. How are you boys, at this ungodly fourth hour of the day? This Half Baked flavor you boys have been cookin' up is getting me happy nappy dappy."

They smiled, as high as kites.

I reached for the pen and ink.

"I'm gonna sit right down and write the revs a letter, and make believe it came from you. . . ."

Dear Reverend Murray,

We are ice cream manufacturers in Vermont, which is a state in the Union, north of the Mason-Dixon line.

We're not sure if you've heard of it down there. It's famous for cows, a socialist congressman, and us.

We're writing this letter to you on behalf of our most addicted customer, who is too baked on painkillers right now to put pen to paper. He wants you to know that his lawn is no longer in peril. And he wants to make it quite clear that the patriotic duty in saving a lawn's life is given the proper acclaim by men of the cloth. He is also having a tooth pulled soon and would like to ask this question for possible reading over the airwaves: Does God put a penny under the pillows of those who have lost their teeth in heaven and are dentures available in purgatory?

Yours socially,
Ben and Jerry

P.S. Our customer wishes to apologize for his last letter when he claimed that he would never write to you fellows again, and that he had abandoned hope. Now he knows that hope springs eternal.

CHAPTER 25

Make Believe

Back in the 1960s and 1970s, the man was a soccer legend. He came from the harsh streets of Belfast. Pelé himself said that he was the greatest European player he had ever seen. Naturally, his name was Best—George Best.

And decades ago, he had spent his twenty-first birthday drinking in the San Francisco pub I now worked in. His ghost lingered there.

I stood on the other side of the bar at closing time. Everyone was gone. It was just George Best's spirit and I. I looked around and tried to imagine where he had stood. Did he sit at a table? Did girls surround him? What did he have to drink?

"George, I know you're here. Send me a message and I'll pass it on."

I saw his famous goals and his wild and mazy dribbling run through my memory. Defenders left twisted like old yarn, goalkeepers splayed like flounders out of water, victims of Best's genius with a soccer ball. And right here in this bar, while visiting America, he had raised a glass legally for the first time but not the last.

"George—give me the spirit. The Dragons need a goal. They need a George Best. They need a god!"

George Best drank himself to death.

• • • •

When I was a kid, listening to soccer commentary on the radio would drive me into spasms of ecstasy. On the dial, the match commentator would scream, "It's a goal!" and in the background the roar of the crowd would take you to the stadium in an instant, and I would leap ten feet in the air and grab my brother and dance wildly, cheering, out of control.

And I was the radio commentator for our street scrimmages, too. Each of my friends would choose to be a star player, but I was always George Best. I would run the commentary from my mouth, celebrating stunning upset goals with a fantastic stretch of clichés interspersed with crowd noises. By the end of the scrimmage, I was hoarse. My pals loved it. They begged me to keep doing it every time we played.

When I first came to America and missed important games back home, my mum would put the phone up to the radio and let me listen to the commentary on her long-distance dime. I wanted the Dragons to feel that power. I wanted them to be inspired by commentary. And if they heard that voice inside their heads when they played the next game, it might inspire them to seek the goal and glory.

At practice, I set up the field for a scrimmage. I split the disciples into two teams of six; one would be England, the other Scotland. Il Duce was missing today, but his son, Speedy Gonzalez, was there. The boy with the blond curls was ready to kick off. He was playing for Scotland and he was the team captain. The potted plant was England's captain.

"And here we are in Berlin for the World Cup Final between Scotland and England. And who would have believed that such a moment would ever occur? These two nations, at each other's throats for centuries, a bitter rivalry. One of them today will be strangled. There are five million kilted Scottish fans inside the stadium, almost the entire nation, and the noise is deafening. And the referee is checking his watch."

I blew.

"The World Cup Final is under way, a huge roar from the crowd."

I did my roar.

"The Scottish captain with the blond curls is on the ball. He moves forward, looking left. He's got it out to Speedy Gonzalez. He's cutting down the wing faster than a bullet. And Manny the England defender makes a great tackle just outside the eighteen-yard box. Throw in to Scotland. Drake takes it; it's a long one into the box but the England keeper is out quick to mop up any danger. A long kick down the field. Here's the England captain Plant making a move."

I blew the whistle.

"It's a free kick to England, a clumsy tackle by Scotland's

right back, Black. Beckham is stepping up to take it. He's checking his hair. It looks superb. Here's the cross from Beckham and . . ."

I made a big *Ohhhhhh* sound.

"He almost got on the end of that, quite remarkable."

"Goal kick to Scotland. Out it goes, picked up in the midfield by the Scotland captain, earning his eighty-fourth cap for his country tonight; he moves into the English half, his blond hair flowing, he's looking for some movement but he goes with pace, he is moving forward, he's looking to shoot and . . . oh, good grief . . . what a savage tackle by England's center half, Manny, an absolute butcher's apron of a challenge. The referee is reaching for his yellow card . . ."

"That's not fair," said Manny.

"Manny, you can't chop our own players down like that," I said, switching back to being head coach. "He's our best player!"

"But you said be hard and that I was playing for England and they are tough."

"No, I didn't say that! English soccer players are a bunch of soft toys. They care more about blow-drying the hair on their toes than they do about being hard."

"I want to play for Scotland then. I hate blow dryers. My dad blow-dries his hair."

"Just get on with playing, Manny. No backchat. We've given up hacking but I might let you hack the enemy on Saturday if you stop being cheeky."

I started my match commentary again.

"Free kick to the Scots, just outside the box. This is a real opportunity. England's goalkeeper, Dolt, is setting up his wall. The captain will take it, through the wall, and . . . *gooooal!!!!* Scotland has scored in the World Cup Final against England."

I quickly blew for full time.

"That's not fair. That didn't last long," said Manny.

"Scotland's waited long enough, Manny," I said. "Hey, did you guys like that commentary?"

"Yeah, it was cool. I thought it was a real game. Can we do it again next time?"

"Of course," I said.

Manny asked, "Who's Dolt?"

"He plays for England," I said.

"And who's Speedy Gonzalez?"

"He plays for Mexico."

"No, he doesn't. He's a cartoon. I've seen it," he said, like the cheeky wee bastard that he was.

With fantasy practice done I pulled the team together.

"Now listen. On Saturday, when you get the ball, imagine that you're a star player and that millions are watching you on TV. Hear the voice of the match commentator in your head. Hear him scream your name when you score that goal. On Saturday, we score. We only have two chances left to do it. We can't be the only team in the history of the world to never score a goal. We don't want to be remembered like that."

"And we're not getting stuck in," said Manny.

The team trotted off to their waiting vans. I took the kid with the blond curls aside.

"I want you to look at this picture," I said.

"Who is that?" he asked.

"It's George Best. He was the greatest player ever. You're George Best."

"I'm the best?"

"You are our best player. I'm making you the team captain of the Dragons," I said.

"What's that?"

"You are the team leader. They follow you on Saturday. It's all up to you now, Besty."

CHAPTER 26

Saturday

nce upon a time, a long time ago, in a faraway land called Hungary, where many people went without food for long periods of time, a man invented a horse-drawn carriage. It was the breakthrough the lazy, rich eighteenth-century aristocrats had been waiting for—a sturdy, solid vehicle equipped with excellent suspension, a perfect solution for the butt-busting journeys those fat bums of the period endured while traveling across the rutted *Bahns* of Europe. The dictionary makers named it after Kocs, the village of its origin. In Germany they called it a *Kutsche;* the French went with *coche;* the Italians traveled in a *cocchio;* and the English climbed into their "coach." Little did the master artisans of Kocs realize that several centuries later, the screwing of nuts and bolts to wheels would result in an invention called John Madden.

No one knows for certain how the word transformed itself from a vehicle to a philosophy and practice. Some etymologists suggest that frequent travelers of yore often took along their sires and tutors, who gave lessons to the children as they sped to and fro from manor to town. Teaching the mobile kids while in the coach became coaching. Alternatively, some linguists suggested a metaphorical root along the lines of successfully getting men along a path. Inevitably, many coaches lost parts along the way. Some jerked, others jumped, making the journey uneven, while others disintegrated, leaving tales of woe scattered across their path.

The etymology of the word "blood" seems perfectly clear—surely it comes from "to bloom." My hands were in bandages. Blood was blooming from the palms.

There was a rope slung over the branch of a tree in a park near my house. The swing swung out over an incline, a nasty drop of six feet for those who let go.

"Let me have a shot," I told my son.

Off I sailed into the void. Each knock in my two-hundred-pound frame suddenly became a ton, and the grip began to slide, one ringlet at a time. That's when there came the smell of palm flesh burning as I sank to the bottom of the rope, and into the pit a distance below.

Ignoring the buckled frame and the twisted ankles, I held my cooked hands to the heavens and wailed liked Jesus.

"Ahhhhh . . . my fucking hands."

Each finger was burned like a ruined hot dog at a barbecue, the fate lines on the palms obliterated, life, death, health, wealth now impossible to read, no future, no hands, no way to find out what lay in store. Moaning in agony, trying to open my front door with keys that stuck to the raw flesh, added to the grief. Finally, water. Creams and lotions soothed the flesh but the stigmata were there for all to see.

Bandaged up, I closed the door of my house gingerly. Out in the yard, the grass was growing. I looked at the cuckoo bird on top of my mailbox. I held the wheel of my tin heap with my fingertips.

It was time to go to our penultimate game of the season.

"Follow the kid with the blond curls," I told my kid in the backseat.

That Saturday, we arrived early. I strolled to the corner flag and tiptoed around the little quadrant that distinguished the markings of the corner. I traced my way to the eighteen-yard box, the scene of so much drama in soccer. A teenager was hanging the net inside the goal. I stood on the goal line looking at the penalty spot, twelve yards away. It was never easy.

I made my way upfield, stopping between the penalty box and the semicircle at the center of the field. The inventive, the sublime, and the grafter with iron legs decided the game here. The monikers of Midfield Maestro and Midfield General were soccer badges of prestige. Every team needed these leaders. I walked to the far end. A ball was resting just outside the box. I juggled it in the air and fired home a volley that scorched the underside of the bar. "Goal!" yelled the teenager finishing off the hooking of the net at the other end of the field.

The Dragons' arrival commenced. Il Duce emerged from his ratty auto, on time, with his boy. The Aztec god, with his daft hippie parent-guardian blinking wildly, emerged from a van with a "No War for Oil" sticker on the bumper. Dr. John, the psychiatrist, put in an appearance, probably to check on the current rate of my deep involuntary knee bends and strangulation gestures. They were in remission. And there was the kid, the one with the blond curls, our hope.

The sunlight was on him.

"Where's he from? How come I didn't notice him at the start of the season?" I asked Il Duce.

"What happened to your hands? They're bleeding," he said.

A man from Central America was pushing a small wagon tinkling with bells, selling ice cream. I snagged a Ben & Jerry's box.

"Welcome to the game, gentlemen of Vermont."

They raised their cones, and I set about them.

"Gather round, team. Dragons, gather round! Here's the plan. Follow him."

I pointed my ice cream at the kid with the blond curls.

"He's the captain. Do as he says. Now get some balls and practice firing them in at Dolt."

"That's not my name," said the Dolt in Need of a Name Change.

"I know. It's a nickname. All soccer players have them. Guess what they called me."

"I don't know."

"Useless. Now get in goal and make some saves today. You're the priest. Save the souls and the goals. Hey . . . hold it, the lot of you. Come back here! You forgot something. Who are ya?"

"The Dragons!"

I went for a wander in the wilderness. As I crossed the field, I noticed its appalling state. My first act in office when I became mayor would be to close the baseball diamonds. The budget for the public parks would be redirected to the construction of soccer pitches. Sports with fewer participants like baseball would have to take second place to the majority sport, soccer.

Today's opponents were of the velvet cushion variety. They were from the wealthier hills that overlooked us sub-urbanites who dwelled in the flatlands. These kids had large spacious toy closets in their homes. College funds were already secured. Dad would not need to ask the government for the $222 death grant to help with funeral expenses if by some rotten luck some horrible disease claimed a family member. These kids loved playing soccer and Dad was more than happy about it. He did not want Junior mixing with the urban crowd with their bad manners and their bling. The moms were having a picnic, pretty tablecloths on the ground, shapely bodies, well trimmed at the spa, no pubes poking out of the leotard.

I decided to infiltrate them, if you know what I mean. I mingled. I ate one of their cucumber sandwiches and smiled at them with my bright and painful teeth. No one stepped backward. They thought I was one of them.

"The other team look really bad today," I said to a soccer mom. "You know, the thing I like about soccer here is that there is never any trouble at it. No hooligans, no nastiness. I've heard that little league baseball is filled with ugliness."

She smiled and attended to her business at hand, the nothingness that she had brought to the great game of soccer.

Her lack of reaction scared me a bit, so I went to stand next to their coach. He had a metal board with movable magnets depicting each player. He was a master in the language of coaching: *Let's show some hustle . . . way to go . . . keep your heads in the game . . . concentrate . . . create space . . . remember what we did in practice . . . and there's no I in team.*

Why had we not thought of a magnetic board with movable magnets? Blame Mahmoud. He was fucking useless. He couldn't organize a raffle in a Catholic school.

The referee was waiting in the center for the players to break into their positions. I walked across the grass toward him with a cucumber sandwich in hand.

"I hope you're going to be fair today," I said to him.

He was a typical oily teenager. And, silent.

"Let me tell you something," I continued. "We've had a shite season and no thanks to the refs, who have been a disgrace to the laws of soccer. So let's make sure that today, you don't join their ranks. I'll be watching you."

I smiled. "Just kidding, son."

One of his pimples went whiter.

The Dragons rushed past me to take up their starting positions. The kid with the blond curls bumped into me. I grabbed his hand, his blue eyes penetrating. Somewhere in another place a dove flew free.

"Take them, big man. You're our best. Find the Holy Grail. Score the goal," I said.

"Yes, sir, I will," he replied.

It was Saturday. It was the day for football. That's what we foreigners called it. That's what I would call it today. As in, the football match kicked off.

The soft touches from the other mob ran around like dandelion seeds parachuting in the air. Our potted plant had a smile on his face. The referee seemed edgy, glancing over in my direction.

"Scythe the daisies," I yelled at Manny.

●　●　●　●

A sphere of influence, the roundness of it, the ball was like the planets. Earth wasn't pigskin shaped; all the skeptics had to do was look at the heavens and see what God's game was. Granted, he gave the round ball varied tongues, with the baseball, the cricket ball, and the girls in the short skirts on the field whacking hard hockey balls. He gave us big gas giants like the Jovian basketball, too. But the perfect immaculate conception of our fertile earth was the soccer ball, soft and hard at the same time, delightfully floated, spinning with atmosphere and promise.

And he was moving through the midfield with it. The glow from his bouncing locks curled into sparkling breaths above him. Crossing the halfway line, he stepped into the

222 • Alan Black

opponents' half and they came to chase him, moving across the grain of the grass—he saw an opening and headed toward the space. Tackles flew. Stop him! But he threw the defenders aside, and a crack of light appeared—the rush of it filled his eyes, and I knew he had seen it, I felt it in the pulse of my vein, Jerusalem, and I followed him through as he made his way into the box, and their keeper came out to block and . . .

Then there was light.

Goooooooaaaaaalllllll!

And the universe shook. And he turned away with hand open, his golden curls shaking off the light in beads of glory.

"He's done it," I said, as the roars went on, the union of the big bang and creation.

THE SPORTING GREEN

THE GOLDEN GOAL

This was not the sporting beat wished for by a writer seeking a Pulitzer Prize. This journalist could pen the report before the game, two days before the kickoff, on Thursday afternoon. The thesaurus is dry. A new raft of negatives would have to be invented to instill some originality in reporting the Dragons' sporting failure, and frankly, who can be bothered? The Dragons are the perfect beat for the hopeless alcoholic writer, still convinced that somewhere at the bottom of the dregs a diamond hides.

Yes, the Dragons lost on Saturday. Yes, the Dragons can't play soccer. Yes, the gas from Coach Black still smells like a badly digested sulfur sandwich. And, O mighty me, yes! The Dragons scored a goal.

And so, a withdrawal from the happy word bank was finally required. There was no need for this journalist to scamper back to the office and pry open a dictionary to find gleeful words and fill his column with miraculous adjectives. The Scottish coach provided the necessary light.

"Ya beauty! We are aglow, beautiful, blessed, blissful, and bright. Celebrate! Be delighted and elated; enjoy this moment with exuberant joy. Hail the invigorating pleasure, scream and laugh and whoop. Raise your hands and yell and grab a person and shake them, and hark the word that a goal has been scored. Morning has broken."

CHAPTER 27

The Chosen Few

I missed the cat, Steven.

And then it was three a.m. Several hours earlier I had called the police from the bar. A sniper with a BB rifle in a high-rise was shooting bar patrons smoking outside on the street. The police never came. They never did.

I grabbed Ben and Jerry and marched them to the sofa. Reverend Arnold Murray was on the throne tonight. Old Testament trouble was brewing as usual. One tribe wading into another tribe, the blood was everywhere. You needed to bring a medical kit, or a MASH unit, to survive the Old Testament. Reverend Murray rarely mentioned Jesus. Jesus was too much of a fairy for the former Marine who had smashed Commie gooks in Korea.

Reverend Murray had an interesting résumé. The reverend's reluctance to accept black people's worth had been attacked, but he seemed to have made efforts to stem the tide of criticism by having a black lady interviewed for his website at one of his Passover gatherings in Arkansas. Some in the evangelical community were scared of him. Once, during a recording of *The Shepherd's Chapel,* he pulled out a nine-millimeter pistol on the air, when a studio invader yelled "Blasphemer" at him. Some said that his Serpent Seed doctrine had Adam shagging the devil. And the horny one had poked his hot rod inside Eve, giving birth to the evil Cain. The Garden of Eden was some kind of bisexual swingers' nudist camp. But what caught my eye was Reverend Murray's belief in something dangerous and odd: British-Israelism.

Way back when, before buses and Eurail cards, the King of Assyria booted out the tribes of Israel, some of whom were doomed to wander the hidden pages of history until they were discovered again by nineteenth-century British snobs keen to suggest that the reason the sun never set on the British Empire had something to do with the fact that the British were the chosen few, that they, the British, were in fact the lost tribes of Israel.

The lineage of the scarlet thread led straight from the House of Judah to Buckingham Palace, where Queen Victoria was on the pot. The reverend claimed that the Celtic tribes were originally from the Black Sea, where the lost tribes had first been scattered. The Romans named Ireland Hibernia. Hibernia started with the letter *H.* So did the word "Hebrew." That was overwhelming evidence right there. The Stone of Scone, an ancient block of wild rock that had been inserted under the throne of the Scottish kings as a symbol of royal power, was also known as Jacob's Pillow. Legend has it that Jacob hauled it with him on his trip to Britannia. No wonder he had a bad back. So the Brits, the Scots, and the Irish were the real Jews, according to Reverend Murray. And by association, so were their descendents in America.

I looked at Ben and Jerry, the half-baked flavor slinking into my coronary chambers and mental fatigue.

"Hey, Ben and Jerry. Did you know that I am part of the chosen few? According to the reverend, if I heard him right. It's written in the Bible and that is why I know we are going to triumph in the final game. I am going to be a winner. And that kid with the blond curls, the one who scored the glory goal, do you know where he is from? Can you guess? Il Duce told me. He's from Israel! He's my brother in arms!"

I was now fully baked.

I looked around for the cat.

I forgot it was dead.

I pulled up my shirt and poked my belly.

"This is going to be a good year, my ice cream friends. I'm going to be a winner at last. Start counting the votes."

• • • •

I was standing at the side of my resurrected lawn chatting to a friend.

"Hey, how did the soccer season go? You were coaching that team—what was it?"

"The Dragons."

"Yeah, that's right."

"One game to play. We have to win."

"Did you win any other games?"

"*Nein.*"

"Nine?"

"Yeah, that's right."

"Wow. You guys were good."

"I'm thinking of going to Germany for the World Cup Finals," I said.

I had forgotten what it was like to win. So you had to lie. But what of that little symbol for victory, the *W*? I wanted it badly in my column. I was sick of the loser letter *L*. It was a dismembered, disabled right-angle triangle. *W* was much better, it worked—Double V, Double Victory. And for electoral popularity, it was a proven two-time winner, fifty million voted for the W. Where could I get a Bush T-shirt with "The Big W" emblazoned on it? I bet they had them down in Arkansas. And then it struck me why Kerry lost. His name started with a *K*. (Strike. You're out.) I dreaded to think what the *C* meant in Clinton.

"Hey, I'm thinking of running for office, maybe becoming the mayor of this green and pleasant hamlet."

"Really. That's very megalomaniac of you," said my friend. "You could be the next governor of California if you play your cards right. Then who knows, constitutional amendment, President?"

"Yes. I've been thinking about using an *A* as my campaign letter."

"Like Asshole? Who's going to vote for that?" he said.

Was that what I had been to these kids? I couldn't get it out of my mind that I had made lips tremble and eyes cry.

How pathetic was that? I was a man towering over boys two feet shorter than me, and talking down to them. And not once had I considered placing myself in their shoes. Were they not supposed to look up to me? And if they had, what would they have seen?—hairy nostrils that needed a trim, is all I could think.

CHAPTER 28

The Emptiness

The Hungarian dentist sent a card. A bright and brilliant bleached set of sunny grippers flashed from the front of it. The back announced the details for my appointment. The tools would be sharpened, and the pliers would be scraped of rusted enamel, ready to pull a crude example of a tooth gone wrong. Would it be recycled, given to the poor who didn't have any teeth? Surely someone could use it.

My teeth had been crippled at an early age. To understand why, you had only to consider the two types of products that were delivered to doorsteps in Glasgow. First, the morning would begin with the clatter of milk bottles arriving, the metal tops pecked open by sparrows. Cornflakes went for a swim, lashings of tea turned milky white, with the bones of the nation well hard. The other delivery came only twice a week. A shadow would draw across the land, and the truck of dental death would roil into the street, loaded with crates of root-rotting soda. The soda company's name was Alpine, and its product was packed with enough sugar to please Havana.

The Alpine bottle was a massive sixty-four-ounce glass soda bomb that exploded with fizz when opened. There was limeade, cola, orangeade, lemonade, and American cream soda, considered by some to be the premium of the batch. I often polished off a half bottle of it while watching Daisy's dukes in *The Dukes of Hazzard*.

On hearing the Alpine truck's rumbling engine belly into the street, kids in the 'hood would gallop to their front doors and jump giddily as the delivery man walked up the path with four bottles gripped in his sticky fingers. Fighting to get the top off first, my brother and I would wrestle. Whoever won the fight would leave a saliva floater in the bottle, preventing the other fiend from partaking anymore from the favored flavor. Alpine sodas taught kids how to be harsh to each other, and how to secure their stash, like drug addicts.

My local dentist was used to dealing with tooth carnage in children. But I liked my teeth. I smiled in the mirror, and then it was wiped from my face and never really came back. It was a most horrible shock.

It happened the day the words "eighteen fillings" came out of the dentist's mouth, and I cried all the way home. My mum called him to check the veracity of the claim. I never found out if the number was correct. I spent months looking at toothless goldfish in a colorful tank and then up the nostrils of a man in a white jacket. I was afraid to look but when I finally did, a corrugated metal testimony shone where my smile used to be. My mum canceled the Alpine delivery, and ordered more milk.

• • • •

I fingered my tooth for the last time as I drove to the surgeon, a little tender stroke on its last journey. I listened to sad classical music as I drove. When I got there, the dentist was speaking Spanish to a Mexican man who had just emerged from the depths of the chair. Cash was leaving his pocket. I looked at the travel magazines; planes were taking off, vacation getaways everywhere, and pictures of departure lounges. The Mexican man shuffled to the door, his mouth swollen, his wallet shrunk.

The doctor smiled and it was a pleasant, Eastern European–style, post-Soviet but still too early to break through the cheeks smile. Only the Yanks could smile from sea to shining sea. The fluorescent lights on the ceiling flashed a beam off the dentist's glasses, the lenses designed to magnify on the lower half.

"Fluorescent. Fluoride. Are they connected?" I said, pointing.

Anything to distract the mind before the medieval torture began.

I looked at the exit, then the chair in the surgery. The getaway promise in the magazine stared up at me.

Smile, I thought. Smile like you mean it.

"Step this way, Alan," she said.

Back I went. The interrogator's lamp swung over my face. Her glasses appeared above, the eyes enlarged by the effects of the strong lenses.

Hungary, I thought. Did they have dentists in Hungary? Did they have teeth in Hungary? Were they a nation of dentists? Wasn't that where Dracula was from? No, that was Romania, or was it?

The lance at the tip of the syringe dripped liquid onto her blue glove.

"Open," she said.

What was it like to be hungry in Hungary? I thought. When bellies rumbled, did people feel a sense of irony?

I acknowledged that being slightly inverted with your mouth open, and another human being fiddling around inside you like a car mechanic, prompted dumb thoughts to fall off the shelves inside your mind.

I heard my tooth's death rattle and final scream.

The panoply of barbaric implements lay in view. Hooks, jabs, pointers, scrapers, designed to make you suffer. The noisy sucker machine swallowed the saliva, and my throat gulped, my eyes half-closed, then wide open to see the executioner's needle descend into the cave to puncture the wall.

Ah.

The phone rang. As I lay back waiting for the numb to ice, I heard the dentist taking an appointment, speaking in fluent French. She had no assistant.

"It's hard to make money in dentistry," she told me when she returned to the surgery. "Numb yet?"

On many levels, but not the one she meant. The needle was loaded again and stuck home. Nothing. Again. Nothing. Again. Nothing. Lower right, second molar was unwilling to die without a fight, putting up a stiff resistance like a partisan. Finally, the mouth grew tired of staying the execution and succumbed to the drugs. The operation commenced.

A contraption was inserted around lower right, second molar. A screw wound it up and away from the rest of its neighbors.

Hungary, I thought. Eastern Europe. Invented the coach.

The blood bloomed around the root. The pliers were reached for. The metal noose grabbed the naked neck of the molar. Slowly, rocking back and forth, a terrible eek-eek sound escaped the cave. I looked up, and a mist rolled over.

The tooth departed.

A part of me was gone.

As I lay there with mouth agape, she spoke to me in a strange tongue. I was bewildered and frightened. Was this the moment the chair crashed backward and I fell through the floor into a mass grave of dental victims, unpolished, the great unflossed?

She burst out in exclamation. "Oh, my God," she said, "I thought I was talking to a Hungarian. Forgive me."

I went dizzy and had to be helped up.

The appointment card was marked return.

"More problems. You're not flossing—we wouldn't want another tooth to go the way of the last one," she said, fangs ablaze.

I played my tongue around the hole. Another loss.

* * * *

At practice, the kid with the blond hair seemed troubled.

"What's up, kid?" I asked him. "That was an amazing goal last week. One of the best I have ever seen."

"Thanks," he said.

"On Saturday, do you think you can score more?"

"Yes. I can score lots, if I feel like it."

"That's the spirit. Do you hear that?" I yelled at the team. "On Saturday he is going to score lots of goals."

"If I feel like it."

"You will feel like it."

"If I feel like it."

I approached Il Duce, who was looking as if he had put on a couple of inches since the last game.

"We're growing in stature. But I'm worried about the boy. He seems removed."

"Yes. He seems a little down in the mouth."

"Okay, Dragons. Come on in. So listen up. Saturday is the last game."

They cheered.

"And we are going to win. This is our last chance. We have to throw everything that we have at the opponents. Everything that we have learned at practice all year."

"Like that 'get stuck in' stuff," said Manny.

"No. Forget that. We don't need that anymore. We've got the talent. We've learned how to pass. We've learned to hold our positions. We've learned to mark up. We cover the posts at corners. We fall back and support the defense. We've learned to hit them on the break. We learned the spirit behind teamwork."

"I can't remember all that," said Manny.

"Manny, you've learned it. That's why you can't remember it!" I said. "Now remember this. Follow the captain. We're going to win. We are not leaving this season without a win. The Dragons are a team that will win. Who are ya?"

"The Dragons," they shouted.

"Now, hold up. Who knows what this is?"

I pulled out a tooth and showed the team.

"It was in here." I opened my mouth. "Now it's out here."

"Put it under your pillow," said the Dolt in Need of a Volt.

"No, here's what I'll do. If you win on Saturday, I'll eat it!"

Wa-hey!

• • • • •

The yard was full green again. Not long enough for the lawn mower yet, but decidedly moving upward. My kid and I could play soccer on it. I'd buy a little goal and he could batter the ball at me before I took him swimming. But before that, he had to take his place in the team for the last game of the season.

The Dockers were pressed, the golf shirt washed, the loafers ready to wade in. I pulled the heap into the car park. I saw Il Duce. He looked troubled, deeply troubled.

"Mahmoud is back," he said.

"What?"

"He's back."

"He can't be!"

"He is."

"You were a great assistant. But, you're fired."

"Hi. How are things going?" I said to the prodigal leader.

"Yes," he said, oddly.

"Where were you, Mahmoud?"

"In L.A."

"Why?"

"Business."

"Business?" I said. "No one told me that you were leaving. You just vanished."

"It was unexpected. I have a mentor there. She needed help. How are things with the team?"

"With my team?"

"Yes, the team?"

"Never better, Mahmoud. Since you left, the team has actually played some soccer. They have actually been coached. They scored a goal."

"Well, good. I'm back now. For the last game."

"There's something on the bottom of your shoe, Mahmoud. I think it might be dog doo."

The bottom line was this. Mahmoud had fucked off and left the team. Not a word of apology. And here we were caught in the web, cell phones, land lines, telegraphs, smoke signals, and was there a call from Mahmoud to his assistant coach saying, "I'm sorry, can you take over the team while I'm off on business? Many thanks, I'll see you at the end of the season." I was livid, bartering my anger at an individual for another prejudicial swipe at a whole culture. But I said nothing more. Resentment brought out the worst in vile thoughts. But there was no escaping it. I simply smiled. Sometimes America was built on false showing.

"Welcome back, Mahmoud."

The praetorian parents on the sidelines aimlessly hobnobbed. What did they care if Mahmoud had usurped the team? It meant nothing to them. Most of them simply turned up at practice, dropped off Junior, and then headed off for ninety minutes of trysts, coffee, massages, tanning beds, cocktails, meetings, shopping, dog walking, or screaming into a pillow. I was the one who had to coach their ungrateful brats. I was the one who had to shake the hand of the opposing coach as he laughed beneath the surface at the loser asshole coach.

I dropped to the ground for the deepest involuntary and final knee bend of the season.

"Did you have fun coaching the Dragons?" asked Dr. John.

"Fun?"

"Yes. Was it fun?"

"Soccer's never been about fun, Doctor."

"It should be."

"No. It's never about fun. Let me ask you this. Do Americans love using the word 'fun' because it's a three-letter word that they can spell, like God and gun?"

Mahmoud was in the center of the field, shaking hands with the referee and the coach from Team Cruz. The players were standing still in a circle, like Stonehenge. The sun struck them and cast a long shadow. The referee blew his whistle for the kickoff, for the last time.

And there was no sign of the kid with the blond curls. I looked at the sky. He wasn't coming. Someone said that they had last seen him on the underground a few days ago, heading toward San Francisco.

At the end of the match, I took the tooth from my pocket. I walked into the penalty box and stood on the spot. It was never easy. I threw it in the air and volleyed it into the net.

• • • •

It was three a.m., for the last time, the day after the rock was rolled away from the cave and I escaped the Dragons. It was Saturday night. At work a few hours earlier, I overpoured the cocktails and slammed the freebies. The fun and happy seekers were rolling in the aisles. Girls were slurring their "likes."

Ben and Jerry were laughing all the way to the bank, as I was getting much fatter on their produce, like a good American should. I pulled out their bitter Irish filling, the black-and-tan flavor left over from a long-forgotten St. Paddy's Day. It hurt my teeth. I opened a can of Ireland's famous stout and waited to start the long journey to the bottom of the glass.

"Cheers, Reverend!" I said. "By the time this settles, Jesus will have come back. Twice."

He couldn't hear me. He was too far away. Plus, he didn't care. This would be the last time I watched *The Shepherd's Chapel*. I didn't need his Old Testament drug to get to sleep. And I was through watching his KFC bucket son with the dodgy mustache barking on about Numbers.

It was time for my final missive to the Arkanshites, an obituary.

Dear Reverend Murray,

One day, when he was growing up on the Dead Sea shores, a young man stopped short and emitted a tiny yelp! A small pebble, round and dried by the salty beach, was burrowing its way into his sole. At first he ignored it and walked on but soon the yelping returned and he had no option but to pry open the flop of his sandal and find the culprit. It had burrowed deep as if it were the snout of an insect intent on anchoring its wedge into his foot. After several hacks with his thumbnail, the miscreant intruder popped out and bounced along the beach. He ran after the rolling stone, his hair brightening in the salon of the sun. He took the stone in his hand. It was perfectly round, shaped by the mold of his sole. "What a beautiful thing," he said. And he raised his foot to kick that annoying bastard of a pebble as far as it would go. He watched as the pebble traveled through the sky, over the sea and beyond, as it screamed to the heavens, and orbited the earth, the sun, the Milky Way, the nearby galaxies, the quadrant, the sector, the black holes, and flung widely by Newton's sling it carried back down to the earth and was known to all as the Pebble Kicked by the Son of a Man, who lived somewhere near a seashore, somewhere where the folks wore sandals.

Word spread amongst the villages and many came and went forth to see the boy with the marvelous kick. In their baskets they brought him the fruits of their trees, and soon he was kicking olives, oranges, and pomegranates into orbit, new constellations of fruits and vegetables adding vitamins to the universe. Wives offered husbands' butts, but here he drew the line.

The word spread to other lands, the angry lands beyond the honey and the oranges, and soon men came from the East with belts on, offering Dynamite, Gelignite, and Steel. A great sadness enveloped the people and the kicker boy left, to head West, and his journey was stop and go, until he reached the off-ramp on Interstate 80 in the land of milk and honeys, called California.

There he joined a team of losers, reprobates, the dull, the deaf, the emotionally rocked, all of them looking for a leader. The High Priests of the team were at odds with each other, squabbling, remonstrating, and sowing the seeds of division with curses and the gnashing of brown teeth. And on this stormy sea he walked and delivered a sermon of grace, a crashing wave of hope that sent his followers higher than a barrel of crude fired from a cannon, sliding through the midfield of banality and mediocrity. He polished that single jewel, and gave the Holy Grail to a team of disbelievers. He scored the only goal. His triumph showed men that there was always hope. That no matter how many clouds sat on the roof of the Lord, no matter how many thunderstorms pelted the hail of loss and doubt to the ground, a single drop of light was stronger than all.

And he came and he went away again and the sentries could not find him. And word spread and his myth grew and soon the land was filled with . . .

The pen expired. I decided not to post it. I would bury it in a time capsule underneath my lawn, and a future generation would dig it up and wonder, what is this rubbish? Is it the Lost Gospel of the Chosen Few?

THE SPORTING GREEN

BACK TO SQUARE ONE

Coach Mahmoud made a dramatic return to the Dragons' bench today, replacing the Scotsman and sending the Italian down to an insignificant footnote in soccer history. The Scoto-Italo era came to an end at the death of the season. And appropriately enough the Dragons played like the team that they are and have been all season long: corpses warmed up.

Missing from the lineup was the kid with the golden curls. Was it some horrible injury? Or had he been transferred to another playing field in a higher division? Was he snatched from his garden and being held prisoner? Was he hanging around somewhere else? The rumors were enough to kick off a religion.

The Dragons missed him. And they were slaughtered. The previous game's promise, the goal, the closeness of the result, was a distant memory. The team returned to the hideous bunching attraction, seeking safety in swarming numbers, like ants depressed by the death of their monarch.

The Dragons' supporters had come to the match in huge numbers. They packed the sidelines. They thought they were about to see the big V sign. Instead, they got the thumbs-down. It was a long journey home for the faithful, a season pregnant with wandering wildernesses, delivering nothing but thorns and much pain in the derriere. The team being down eight–nil at halftime, many of the fans left for the exits after their pee. Loyalty is a thin wafer in soccer, a melted vanilla, a chubby hubby, and a chunky monkey of disappointment. Ben & Jerry's ice cream was today's match sponsor but the flavor was rancid for the Dragons, and the flow of goals shredded their defenses.

The Dragons went down like a balloon on Mercury. The Cruz, punishing with their hot winged fleet of fancy footwork, danced and dribbled their way to their largest win of the season. With the Dragons drying up like a thirsty camel in the desert, the final whistle put the season over the hump, extinguishing the Dragons and the ludicrous comparisons.

CHAPTER 29

The Pizza Party

The postseason pizza party for the Dragons and their parents took place in the hills above the flatlands. Once up there, I parked and breathed heavily; I was not used to this rarified atmosphere. Below me was the rest of the world. I noticed that my tires needed inflation. It was nice of a parent to offer to host the defeated. They were rich.

Like exhibits in a Western museum, large cartwheels of cheese and pepperoni pizza were laid out in the remarkable kitchen. There were marble countertops, fancy faucets, not a crumb on the floor, no mold inside the bread bin that looked oddly like Sputnik. Bowls of blue corn chips, corn tortillas, and guacamole were on offer. Lashes of sodas were strung out for the kids, sparkles of mineral water for the recovering alcoholics or the responsible driving class, and chilling beer and sweet wines for the adults who could handle getting behind the wheel after a few. There was a sense of having to tread carefully. Dropping a plate might trigger an alarm. Use the correct bathroom after eating the hot chilies.

In the back garden I saw that there was a tree swing. I felt a sting stab my hands. Was that a Jacuzzi in its gazebo waiting to gurgle hot bubbles up the bums of naked parents as they suckled champagne grapes?

The dog barked. It ran up to me and started sniffing my Dockers crotch.

"There's no life in there, Bozo," I said.

The phone rang. An American football game was on the telly. Dads were calling plays. The shuffle of loafers and the crimp of khakis passed through the enormous living room. A radio station was smoothing jazz into the mix.

Touchdown!

The men moved to baseball and talked averages. That summed it up.

The Dolt's dad spotted me and handed me a bottle of Beck's and a strong handshake.

"I don't know anything about soccer," he said. "Do you have any good golf stories?"

"As a matter of fact, I do. If it were not for golf I would not be standing here now talking to you. I would never have been the coach, the head coach, of the Dragons."

"Really," he said.

"Yes, really. I came to this country without the proper paperwork. I was detained at Houston airport. They put me in a windowless room and there was a big sign on the door that read EXIT. I was sweating buckets. An immigration cop came in and said, 'What's the story, son?' I told him I forgot to bring the paperwork. 'That's not how it works,' he replied.

I thought I'd be back in Scotland by nightfall. And then he asked me where I was from. 'Scotland,' I said. I noticed his name tag. Campbell. It didn't get more Scottish than that. I thought about mentioning my favorite was Cream of Mushroom but then he said, 'I've always wanted to play eighteen at St. Andrews.' 'Beautiful course.' I saw my only chance. 'Drive right on the sixteenth. Stay out of the rough on the fourteenth.' His eyebrows rose up. The door opened. I was in. 'Welcome to America,' he said, in a fake Scottish accent."

"Well, that's an amazing story," said the Dolt's dad. "We should go out for eighteen sometime."

"I hate golf," I said. "Do they have golf in Iran?"

Groups of parents were swarming around Mahmoud. He was happy among these people. He could speak of business success and other inane cack. He was part of this, free from bigotry and suspicion. He swigged bottled water. I cracked open another Beck's, one in each hand. I rotated around Mahmoud and the parents. Their backs were toward me. I could hear cold shoulders of ice crackle in their glasses.

The lavatory was a sunglasses job. The sparkle of the inner pan was glorious; an excellent canvas for a Jackson Pollock–inspired Bovril abstraction. I tried the faucets for instant hot water, and like a waterfall it swished around the ceramic before the black hole gobbled it. I opened the door of the shower, big enough for two to screw. I flushed the lavatory twice. What a waste. I peered out the bathroom window. I could hear Mahmoud. I rolled a knob of toilet paper in my hand, put it under the water, then stepped back and threw it out the window. I was sure I heard a slight splodge. Maybe it landed on Mahmoud's head.

Back at the party someone I didn't recognize was opening the dishwasher. The clink of the plates, likely gifted from the wedding registry, was barely audible. I wandered to the deck. A soccer ball was there. I flicked it up and fired it into the garden.

Il Duce was standing in a corner, barely higher than a vase. His mood was somber. The breeze picked up. I didn't want to get too close in case flecks of his blustery dandruff peppered me.

"Well, it was a rough season," I said.

"Disastro!"

"Yes. It was disastro. Are you putting your boy in a team next year?"

"He never wants to play soccer again."

"Mine, too. Pretty sad affair, the sons of Italians and Scots not wanting to play soccer. I guess that's America. By the way, I thought Mahmoud's second coming was bullshit."

I turned and saw the Dragons' potted plant standing among the flowers. Good spot. Out in the garden, Manny was swinging from the tree swing. I gave him the Tarzan impression. He ignored it. The Aztec god had a smile on his face, relieved that there would be no more soccer and he could get back to more important matters, like going quietly deaf.

His guardian came up, wine in hand.

"Well, did you have fun?"

"I had lots of fun coaching the team. I really wanted to give back to my community by giving up my valuable time to coach youngsters. And they were a great bunch of kids. I think your boy has a real future in soccer. He's a great kid, and he was a real joy to work with. Such a good listener."

"That's very kind of you to say. At times I thought you were not having much fun. We didn't see you smile much."

"Well, that's because my teeth were brown. Now they're white!"

Zing!

I went on, "No. It was a fantastic fun experience for me. Awesome really. I'll vote for fun anytime," I said, shaking her hand, a little too tightly.

The refrigerator freezer hummed and spat out endless chunks of ice into the kids' glasses of pop. The Rastafarian was off in a corner staring at the CD collection as if in a trance. I saw the Dolt's dad approach and speak to him. They looked up and saw me staring at them. I felt intrusive.

I grabbed my kid and left without saying good-bye. I looked back and felt a burst of loathing. I formed my mouth into an incipient fu** shape but I didn't follow through. It was time to pave over the curses with concrete.

As I drove back to the lowlands, I put Pink Floyd in the deck: *The Wall*, "We Don't Need No Education." Kids loved that song. And there was a lesson in it for youth sports.

As a kid, no one had taught me to play soccer. I learned it playing with other boys. We organized the game ourselves, and some of us went on to be good. I could only conclude from my coaching experience that when adults and children hung out with each other, and shared innocuous sporting destinies, spilled blood was a strong possibility. Adult-run youth sports should have been banned a long time ago.

Adults had pickpocketed kids' identities, thrown them together in teams without their consent. The kids had become agents for their parents' desires, bricks in the wall of parental hysteria, on the receiving end of adult criticism and dark sarcasm. No wonder so many kids grew up to wear black.

The solution was obvious. Take the kids to the fields and tell them to sort it out for themselves. And they will. Kids know how to organize, they have imaginations and they understand the natural order of leaders and followers. Parents will be forced to watch from a distant raised platform. They must be out of earshot. Teams will play better, players will be happy, and the crisis in kids' sports will be over. And there will be no need for referees. Kids don't need them. Adults do. So the ref can sit with the parents on the platform and hand out yellow and red cards to the bitching moms and blathering dads.

Leave those kids alone.

EXTRA TIME

Born Again on the Fourth of July

It was time for the haircut, a short back and sides. A few months ago, I would have been giving it a sweep over with straggly strands hiding the bald patches and the scabs. But that was before the Lawn Club for Men came into the picture and my garden muscle sprang erect. This would be the first time my reborn lawn would be mowed. It needed the Sunday best for the barbecue on the Fourth of July.

The Scotts lawn mower went into operation. For fun, I cut a German helmet shape in the middle and then plowed over it in liberating waves. At cruising speed, the shave cut clean. My Stars and Stripes T-shirt fluttered in the breeze. Old Glory was on the flagpole. Someone driving down the street would not have been mistaken had they cried out loud, "Look. A homeowner is cutting his grass. That's odd."

The neighbor across the street was having his Fourth of July party in his backyard, hidden from society. I could see the rising smoke signals from his grill.

"Coward," I yelled.

Soon, my friends would be over, standing on my front lawn. I thought about inviting Il Duce. But no—it would relight the evanescent Dragons breath, now reduced to the last word at a funeral, dust. I pulled the Weber to the grass. Abattoirs of meat, coops of chickens, sties of swine, and many fish with scales would feed the five who bothered to show up and see the miracle that had grown beneath their feet.

"This lawn was as dead as a tombstone in a spaghetti Western," I told a friend.

"I know," he said. "I said you were a poor sod. How did it recover?"

"Faith."

"Faith?"

"Yes, Faith. And some seed, fertilizer, and water with some golf shoe action. I took a picture of it today. I'm sending it in to *Lawn and Leisure*."

"Hey, how did that soccer team you were coaching work out?"

"Didn't you already ask me that?"

"No, I don't think so. Did you win?"

"*Nein.*"

"Well done."

I looked at the flag.

"Things just keep repeating themselves, over and over again," I said.

The sound of the suburbs.

"Hey, you don't usually wear those kind of pants, do you?" said my pal.

"I do now," I said. "I'm not planning on having any more kids."

THE SPORTING GREEN

EXTRA-LATE EDITION
BLACK RESIGNS AS DRAGONS' COACH

At a hastily arranged press conference, the Dragons' assistant coach, Alan Black, announced his resignation from the coaching staff. Surrounded by his attorneys and agent, he delivered an emotional statement and then took a question from the press.

"I have notified the team, Coach Mahmoud, and the league of my decision to resign from the position of assistant coach of the Dragons. It has been a marvelous experience and I want to sincerely thank the players and Coach Mahmoud for their utter professionalism throughout a difficult campaign. I would also like to thank Il Duce for his support lower down the rung. Indeed, it is at the bottom that you find the real heroes in life, and the great hope that never dies among losers. In the dirt, in the mud, in the gravel, where the balls are kicked, so much beauty exists. And this has been the most valuable lesson for me this season. It is at the bottom of the league that a coach can find the most happiness. For here you get to believe that one small step is big enough. Spaceman Neil Armstrong, a fellow Scottish American, would have been proud of the Dragons, a team stuck at the foot of the ladder but willing to step off and make their imprint on the field of dreams every weekend, hoping that one small step might lift them up that little bit higher. The Dragons were pioneers, pioneers who struggled and saw the candle burn just once, to perish in the memory, lost in the ocean of all the goals ever scored, but there, there, in that great net, our goal is recorded, my goal, my glory as coach!"

At this point in the press conference, Coach Black sprang leaks in his eyes and blew his nose into a white handkerchief. He threw it at the assembled journalists.

"That's what you've wanted all along, you gentlemen of the press—surrender. Well, you did not get it. I fought to the bitter end, just to spite you vultures. And now I'll take a few questions."

Only one question was asked.

"Coach Black, will you swear that you will never again coach little league?"

"F***ing right I will. And let me say this. I'm moving on to higher office. I'm planning to run for mayor of my hometown because the people need to know what life is like on the scrap heap. So today I announce my candidacy for office. I am ready to get stuck into the problems facing my city. Potholes beware. And let me finish by saying that I look forward to meeting my cheeky bastard press critics in a dark alley one day. Don't forget to wear your shin guards."

Acknowledgments

My mum, who gave me the love of soccer; my brother in arms, Kenneth; and my sister, Valerie. And thanks to David Henry Sterry for keeping me in the game and Danielle Svetcov and Luke Dempsey for the straight shooting. And to all my mates.

About the Author

Alan Black is a bartender by trade. His writing has appeared in the *San Francisco Chronicle*, Salon.com, and the *Christian Science Monitor*.